# 609 LET TEMPLATES AND CREDIT REPAIR SECRETS

## HOW TO FIX YOUR CREDIT SCORE AND TURN A BAD ONE INTO A GOOD AND HIGH ONE

### ERIC CALLAGHAN

# TABLE OF CONTENTS

# INTRODUCTION

Credit is like a report card telling you how well you have paid your bills. Credit is a record of how you pay your credit cards bills, auto loans, mortgage loans, etc. Whenever you buy something with a monthly payment, the people who you collect your bill report this information to create a credit report. Examples include buying furniture on credit or using a Best Buy store card to purchase a computer. Exceptions include utility bills, cell phone bills, and rent payments. Collection accounts, court judgments where you owe money, and bankruptcies are also part of your credit.

A credit report is a document that shows all the information collected by the credit bureaus. A "tri-merge" or "merged" credit report contains the information from all three credit bureaus in one report. This report lists all your past credit accounts that have been reported to the credit bureaus. The report lets you know how much money you owe to creditors, what your available balance is, and your complete payment history, including any late payments. The credit report can

also list your current and former addresses and even employers. Additionally, the credit report will also give you a number that each credit bureau assigns to you, called a credit score.

Credit score is a measure of your financial health. It cannot be affected by external parties (save for filling in actual financial information related to you) and is unbiased. Your credit score is personal information and is not available to anybody and everybody that can use Google search. Rest assured that your personal credit history is not randomly bouncing around the Internet unless you choose to make it publicly available.

Note that if somebody other than you uses your personal information to obtain your credit score without your permission, you can take legal action. You can sue for $1000 or actual damages incurred, whichever is greater.

A credit score can, however, be accessed by legitimate parties as and when necessary. As such, it can be (and usually is) used by several companies and institutions when deciding whether to offer you their services or not.

Your credit score is checked any time you apply for some kind of loan. It includes everything from student loans to housing and car loans. Potential employers, insurance companies, landlords, and utility companies also have access to this information. So do several government agencies. They may use it to get your contact information, determine if you have unclaimed income, see how much you can afford in child support, and much more. Your credit score is used to determine how worthy (or truthful) a credit customer you are. Potential lenders and service providers use it to calculate how

much of a risk you present to them as a borrower. Legal entities will use it to determine how to take action consistent with the laws involved.

Credit repair is the process in which credit standing is fixed, which might have declined due to various reasons. Credit standing might be as straightforward as disputing the information.

Another kind of credit fix is to take care of financial problems such as budgeting and start to deal with concerns.

Significant Points to consider

-Credit repair is the action of repairing or restoring a bad credit rating.

-Credit repair may also entail paying a company to get in touch with the credit agency and point out anything in your report that is untrue or incorrect, then requesting this to be eliminated.

# CHAPTER 1

# FICO

## What is Fico?

Fair Isaac Corporation — the business that produces "FICO" ratings — is the oldest and most omnipresent credit scoring agency. Fair Isaac claims over 80 per cent of investors use their ratings. Factors considered by Fair Isaac as credit scores come up include:

- Payment history (about 35% of the score). The company is looking at things like whether you have paid on time, have any overdue payments, declared bankruptcy, how current past due accounts are, or if you have rulings against you. This is the bulk of your score so it's the most important. Late payments, settlement claims, settled accounts, repossessions, foreclosures, and public record issues such as tax liens, convictions, or bankruptcies can have a significant negative impact on your FICO score, according to Fair Isaac. And even getting a payment just one month late can hurt your ranking.

- Amounts owed on credit accounts (about 30% of the score). Fico at things like the amounts that you be obliged, and how many of your accounts hold a balance. The more you owe the lower your score, compared to your credit limits. The principal way to improve this part of your score is to pay down your outstanding debt. Your credit history has a period of around 15 percent of the score. A longer credit history usually yields a higher ranking.

- New credit (about 10% of the score). Fair Isaac wants to see a credit history built, rather than a lot of new accounts. Opening up multiple accounts in a short time may mean a higher risk. Depending on the reason, hard

enquiries about your account may also lower your score. Of example, if a variety of borrowers reviews your credit report it might seem like you are actively applying of new credit. That is why, when shopping for new credit, it is important to be careful. Above all, used car dealers always want to get you to sign a form that requires them to peek at your credit report, even if you're just shopping in the store. Don't consider that until you are adamant about agreeing. But as long as you're doing all of your car or home mortgage comparison shopping within about 30 days or so, it shouldn't have a lot of effect on your ranking. Don't think about enquiries too much. Inquiries make up just a small fraction of your FICO score. According to FICO, the number of requests is typically not a major factor in your credit score— an investigation will probably lower your score by less than 5 points, even if outside a small shopping window for reference. So FICO states that once the investigation is longer than 12 months it does not include inquiries in its ratings.

- Types of credit (about 10% of the score). Fair Isaac is offering a "healthy mix" of different credit forms, including revolving loans (such as credit cards) and maintenance plans (such as a mortgage or car loan). You can see that about 65% of your FICO score depends on whether you pay your bills on time (35%) and whether the balance you owe is too high for your credit limits (30%). You may have more than one FICO score as Fair Isaac now provides several FICO rating models that highlight different aspects of your performance. And because a FICO score is dependent on your credit report,

and each of the three national credit reporting agencies may have very different information on you, the ratings may vary from each of the three organizations.

## What Is a Good FICO Score?

FICO scores range between 300 and 850. Fair Isaac reports that just fewer than 40% of Americans have more than 750 FICO ratings, which most borrowers would find very strong. Equifax claims most FICO scores usually fall between the 600s and 700s and offers these estimates:

- 20% are above 780

- 20% are in the range of 745–780

- 20% are in the range of 690–745

- 20% are in the range of 620–690

- 20% are below 619.

Fair Isaac offers a free calculator that you can use to see how different credit ratings can influence how much you're getting credit for. Go to www.myfico dotcom and click "Education," then "Credit Basics," then scroll down on the left and click "Improve Your Score," then click on "See how much money you can save" in the article.

Most Common Reasons for Negative Credit Decisions

Underneath are the most common reasons for negative credit decisions, according to Equifax. You can see how these fit in with the way you score credit files.

- Serious offence.

- Extreme delinquency, and a filed or triggered public record.

- It is too new or uncertain since the offence.

- The level of accounts criminality is too high.

- The percentage of delinquency accounts is too high.

- Money owed too high on deposits.

- The percentage of credit-limit balances to revolving accounts is too high.

- The length of time the accounts is set is too short.

- Too many balance-accounts.

## The FICO Scoring Model

FICO holds the distinction of most reliable scoring model thanks in no small part to its longstanding track record. Fair Isaac Company began computing these scores back in 1989. They have since revised the algorithms several times in the past over three decades to adjust for shifting factors so that they produce continuously dependable credit scores.

As we noted earlier, the traditional FICO score model will produce a score for you from 300 to 850. Scores of less than 600 equate to poor. If your score is higher than 740 then this is deemed to be excellent.

The ranges in between 600 and 740 mean from average to above average credit worthiness.

In 2014, FICO introduced its FICO 9 scoring model. The primary revision in this model was to reduce the importance

of unpaid medical bills. The reasoning behind this is that medical debts that are not paid are not truly financial health indicators.

You might be waiting for insurance to pay a medical bill or simply be unaware that a medical bill had been given over to a collection agency. For some people, this important change allowed their credit score to increase by up to 25 points.

Other changes in 2017 stopped collectors from reporting late medical debts that were not yet 180 days delinquent. Year 2017 also saw the three credit reporting bureaus drop all of their data on civil judgments and the tax lien records from their files. FICO reported that this helped the scores of around six percent of consumers.

Before FICO 9 came out, FICO 8 (that the company developed in 2009) was the standard credit score version. FICO 8 remains the most commonly utilized score of the lending industry. FICO 8's distinguishing features were to penalize you for charging near your total credit limit each month and to provide compassion if you had only a single late payment of over 30 days.

It is worth noting that each time FICO releases an updated version on its scoring models, lenders may keep the version they are using or upgrade. FICO 8 has remained the overwhelming favorite simply because it costs so much to upgrade to the new model. There are lenders still using even FICO 5 models.

You can ask your lender which model they are using when you go through the application process.

FICO scores typically do not change that much over the short term. The exception is if you start missing payments or showing charge offs and defaults. Not everyone has a FICO score either. If you have no credit, you will fall into the category of what experts call "credit invisible."

You must have six months of payments reported to the credit bureaus to have a FICO score.

# CHAPTER 2

## CREDIT MYTHS

**M**ost people think certain things need to happen to have a great credit score. Most of these myths are wrong and affect their potential to have the highest score possible. Knowing what is true and what is a myth could save you years of mismanaged credit. Focus on reality and not on myths by going over some of the most common misconceptions shown below:

If you are twenty one years old or younger, you can't have a credit score above 700

Wrong. Your credit score is not age based and it does not take this criteria into account when calculating your score.

If I get married, my credit score will go down

Wrong, your credit score is independent to your spouse's score unless you have joint credit accounts in which case payment history and the amount of debt carried can affect you positively or negatively. Your marital status is irrelevant.

If I pay off all my credit cards I will have an 800 credit score

Incorrect. Paying off your credit cards should increase your credit score but there are more factors to take into account when determining your credit score such as: length of credit history, credit mix, inquiries, debt capacity, etc.

If I check my credit online, it will go down

There are instances when having your credit checked or when you check your credit that you're credit scores will not be affected. Normally, your credit score is affected when you apply for credit and your credit is pulled, not when you check your credit.

If I lose my job, my score will go down

This is not correct. Your employment status is not linked to your credit and will not affect your credit score. If you are late on payments as a result of losing your job, this will result in a lower score. If you can keep making your payments on time your score will not go down.

If I make a million dollars a year, I will have a credit score above 750

No. Your credit scores are not affected by how much you make. Your salary can be $100 or $1,000,000, your score will not change. Managing your credit properly will affect your credit. Some very wealthy people can have low credit scores while someone who is getting paid minimum wage can have an over 800 credit score.

If I buy a house worth $700,000 and owe $600,000 my credit will be negatively affected because of the amount of debt I owe

This is not correct. Applying for a mortgage will lower your credit scores because they are being pulled to check your credit but the amount you owe is irrelevant. Your monthly payment can be $4,000 on your mortgage and your credit will not be affected. Once you start paying down your $600,000 loan, your credit will improve as a result of paying on time and lowering you debt. If you put 10% or 30% down payment on a house you buy, your credit will not be affected by this either since it is payment history based and will only be affected by your capacity to repay the loan.

If I move to another country my credit score will go down

It doesn't matter where you live, credit history and your credit score is based on your capacity to manage debt properly not on where you are. You can live in New York City, Miami, Seattle, Washington D.C., Los Angeles, Mexico, Germany, Australia, and your credit score will not be affected.

If I turn 80 years old I will no longer be able to improve my credit score

Wrong, age is not a factor when it comes to your credit and your credit score. If you live to be 120 years old, you can continue having great credit and a high credit score.

If I make a late payment on my credit card my score will drop to 300

Incorrect, assuming a score based on a late payment is not the way to assess your credit score as it can be slightly lower or it can drop much lower. There is no precise way to know exactly what your score will be.

If I apply for too many credit cards my score will go down

Correct. Credit inquiries lower your credit score by a small amount but when you continually apply for credit, your credit will be checked often and will result in a lower score.

# CHAPTER 3

# HARMING MY CREDIT SCORE

It is also necessary to take a closer look at some of the different parts that are going to end up harming the credit scores that we have. If you are in the process of fixing your credit, you want to make sure that you are careful and that you are not going to end up doing something that will harm your credit in the process. Some of the different things that we can watch out for when it comes to harming your credit score include:

## Paying Late or Not at All

One of the worst things that you can do when it comes to your credit score is paying late on anything. About 35 percent of your score is going to be about your history of making payments or not on time. Consistently being late on these payments is going to cause a lot of damage to your credit score. Always pay your bills on time, especially your credit card bills.

What is even worse than paying late is not paying at all. If you decide to completely ignore your cards and other bills and not pay them at all, then you are going to be in even more trouble as well. Each month that you miss out on a payment for your credit card, you are going to end up with one month closer to helping your account be charged off.

If you ever want a chance to get your credit score up at all, especially if you are hoping to get it up to 800 or higher, hen you have to stop the late payments. This is going to be a bad thing because it shows that you are not willing to pay your money back, and they are less likely to give you some more money in the process.

For those who are struggling with making payments, whether these payments are often late or they don't come in at all, it is time to get a budget in place. You are living above your means, and this is never a good sign to getting your score up to where you would like. When you can get your budget in place and can start paying your debts on time, you will be able to get that credit score higher in no time.

## Having an Account Charged Off or Sent to Collections

Next on the list is having your accounts charged off. When creditors are worried that you will never pay in your bills for loans or credit cards, they are going to use a process known as charging off your accounts. A charge off means that the insurer has pretty much given up on ever hearing from you again. This does not mean that you are no longer going to hold responsibility for this debt at all. This is actually one of

the absolute worst things out there when it comes to your credit score.

Another issue is when one of your accounts is sent off to collections. Creditors are often going to work with debt collectors in order to work on collecting a payment out of you. Collectors could send your account to groups after, but sometimes before, charging it all off. This is never a good thing, no matter if the account is charged off at that time, either.

If you are to the point of your bills going to collections or being charged off, this means that you have not just missed one or two payments. It means that you have gone so long without paying the whole thing that the company figures they are never going to get it back. They have probably either written it off as a tax break, or they have sold it to a credit collection company that will be bothering you a lot in the future.

## Filing Bankruptcy

This is a bit extreme that you should try to avoid at all costs. Bankruptcy is an extreme measure, and it is going to cause a lot of devastation to the score that you are working with. It is also going to be on your record for seven to ten years. It is a good idea to seek some alternatives, like working with counseling for consumer credit, before filing bankruptcy.

It is best if you are able to do everything that you can to avoid bankruptcy at all costs. It may seem like the best idea to work with. You assume that when you declare bankruptcy, you can just walk away from all of the debt that you have, and not have

to worry about it ever again. This is not really how this whole process is going to work for you at all, though.

To avoid bankruptcy, you need to go through and learn how to work with a budget and figure out the best ways to manage your money, no matter what the income is that you are working with. This is easier to manage than you may think and can help you to get on a reasonable payment schedule so that you can deal with your debts and get them paid off. The bankruptcy seems like an easy way to get out of the debt, but it haunts you for many years afterward, can make getting credit later on almost impossible, and it will really not solve the underlying problem that got you to this situation.

## High Balances or Maxed Out Cards

We always need to take a look at the balances that we are going to have on our credit cards all of the time. The second most important part that comes with our credit score is the amount of debt that is on them, and that is going to be measured out by credit utilization. Having high balances for credit cards, relative to the credit limit that you are working with, will increase the use of credit and will make your credit score goes down. For example, if you have a limit of $10,000 on a card, but the balance is at $9500 or higher, then your score is not going to reflect in a positive manner with this one.

We also need to make sure that we are not maxing out or going over the limit when it comes to our credit cards. Credit cards that are over the limit or that have been maxed out are going to make the credit utilization that you have at 100 percent. This is going to be one of the most damaging things

that you are able to do with your credit score. Make sure to pay down those debts as fast as you can to maintain your credit score and keep it from going over the top.

## Closing Credit Cards

There are a few ways that closing your card is going to end up with a decrease in your credit score. First, we need to take a look at closing up a card that still has a balance on it. When you close that card, the credit limit you get to work with is going to end up at $0, while your balance is still going to be the same. This is going to make it look like you have been able to max out the credit card, which is going to cause your score to drop a bit. If you want to close your account, then you need to make sure that you pay off the balance before you close it.

What will happen when you close out your credit cards that are old is another thing to study. About 15 percent of your credit score is going to be the length of your credit history, and longer credit histories are going to be better. Closing up old cards, especially some of the earliest maps, are going to make your account seem like it is a lot shorter than it is. Even if you do not use the card anymore, and there are no annual fees, and you should keep the card open because you are really losing nothing and gaining more.

And finally, we need to be careful about closing cards that have available credit. If you have more than one credit card to work with, some that have balanced and some without these, then closing the cards that do not have a balance is going to increase the credit utilization. You can just keep those all out of the way, and see your credit report go up.

# Not Having Enough Mix on the Report

While this is not as big of a deal as some of the other options, you will find that having a good mix of credit is going to be about 10 percent of your credit score at the time. If you have a report that only has one or two things on it, such as either credit cards or loans, then it is likely the score you are working with will be affected in some way or another.

The more that you are able to mix up your accounts and get them to have a lot of different things on them, the better. You don't want to overextend yourself, but having a mix of loans, mortgage, credit cards, and more, that you pay off each month without fail, is going to be one of the best ways that you can raise your credit score without causing harm or paying too much in the process.

This does not mean that you should go out and apply for a bunch of different things all at once in order to get your mix up. This is something that often happens; naturally, the longer you work on your credit score. You may have a few credit cards. And then you take out a loan for a car and pay it off. Maybe you need a loan for a vacation or for some home improvement so you will have those accounts. And then get a mortgage too.

# Applying for Too Much

Another thing that is going to count on your report is the credit inquiries. These will take up about 10 percent of the score that you work with. Making several applications for loans and credit in a short amount of time is going to cause a

significant drop in your credit score along the way. Always keep the requests for credit to a minimum, so this doesn't end up harming you along the way.

In some circumstances, this is not going to harm you too much. For example, if you have a good credit score and you want to apply for a mortgage, you will want to use for a few mortgages and shop around a bit. If you do these close together, then it is not going to be seen as bad because the lender will assume this is what you are doing, rather than you taking on too much or that you have been turned down. You can also explain this to them quickly if they ask.

# CHAPTER 4

## STEPS TO FIX YOUR CREDIT SCORE

Improving your credit score can mean qualifying for lower financing costs and better terms. That is genuine whether you need a decent credit score to acquire cash for individual reasons or so you can buy stock, rent an office, and so on., to begin or develop your business.

The issue is, credit fix is similar to improving your expert system: You possibly consider it when it is essential. However, if you don't have excellent credit, it's almost painful to address that circumstance short-term.

That is the reason an opportunity to begin fixing your credit is currently - before you genuinely need it.

Luckily, it's not to difficult to improve your credit score.

Here's a necessary procedure you can follow:

1.  Audit your credit reports.

The credit authorities - TransUnion, Equifax, and Experian - are required to give you a free duplicate of your report once every year. You should simply inquire. (Snap the connections to demand a copy.)

Another approach to see your credit reports is to utilize a free assistance like Credit Karma. (I'm not supporting Credit Karma. I like it and believe it's convenient, however I'm individual other free administrations are similarly as valuable.)

When you've joined, you can see your credit scores and view the data contained on the reports. As a rule, the passages on the different stories will be the equivalent, however not generally. For an assortment of reasons credit reports are infrequently indistinguishable.

2.  Debate negative imprints.

In the past times, you needed to compose letters to the credit departments if you needed to question blunders. Presently benefits like Credit Karma (once more, I'm not supporting CK and just reference it because I've utilized it) let you contest blunders on the web.

Simply ensure you get the most blast for your debate endeavors. Certain variables gauge more vigorously on your credit score than others, so focus on those things first.

Start with critical imprints like assortment records and decisions. It's normal to have at any rate one assortment account show up on your report. I had two from medicinal services suppliers I utilized subsequent to having a

cardiovascular failure; my insurance agency continued asserting it had paid while the suppliers said it had not, and in the long run the records wound up with an assortment organization. In the long term I chose to pay the suppliers and contend with the insurance agency later, however the two assortments ended up on my credit report.

Fixing those issues was simple. I tapped the "Contest" button, chose "The creditor consented to evacuate my obligation on this record," and inside seven days the debate was settled and the passage was expelled from my credit report.

3. Contest inaccurate late-installment sections.

Errors occur. Your home loan bank may report an installment was late that was in actuality paid on schedule. A credit card supplier may neglect to enter a chapter accurately.

You can contest late installments - regardless of whether in accounts that are present or records that have been shut - a similar way you debate deprecatory imprints.

Your installment history is another factor that weighs vigorously on your credit score, so make a substantial effort to tidy up those mistakes.

4. Choose if you need to play the game some credit fix organizations play.

So far we've talked about attempting to expel off base data as it were. You can, if you pick, likewise debate exact data.

For instance, say a record went to assortment, you never paid it, and the assortment organization surrendered. All that remaining parts is the passage on your credit report. You can

even now decide to debate the segment. Numerous individuals do. What's more, in some cases those segments will get evacuated.

Why? When you enter a question the credit authority requests that the creditor verify the data. Some will. Many, similar to assortment offices, won't. They'll basically overlook the solicitation - and if they do disregard the tender, the office is required to expel the passage from your credit report.

This means littler firms, similar to assortment organizations or nearby loan specialists or little to average size specialist organizations, are less inclined to react to the credit departments. It's an issue they needn't bother with. Banks, credit card organizations, automobile fund organizations, and home loan moneylenders are much bound to react.

So if you need - and I'm not suggesting this, I'm trying to say it's a system a few people choose to utilize - you can contest data in the expectation the creditor won't react. (This is the methodology many credit fix firms use to attempt to improve their customers' scores.) If the creditor doesn't react, the passage gets expelled.

Would it be a good idea for you to adopt this strategy? That is up to you. (You could contend I shouldn't make reference to it, however it is something numerous individuals do, so I felt it worth referencing.)

5.   Ask pleasantly.

Possibly you attempted and neglected to evacuate a negative remark, a late installment, or a record that was checked "Paid as concurred" (which may mean the creditor consented to let

you pay short of what you owed). Would it be advisable for you to surrender? Not a chance. Take a stab at asking pleasantly.

Creditors can educate credit agencies to expel sections from your credit report whenever. For instance, I hadn't charged anything on a specific credit card for quite a long time and didn't see that I had been charged my yearly expense until the installment was late. (Like a good for nothing, I was simply hurling the announcements without opening them because I "knew" there were no charges.)

The late installment appeared on my credit report, so I called the credit card organization, clarified what had occurred, that I had been a client for quite a long time, and inquired as to whether they would expel the section. They said sure. Furthermore, they additionally consented to forgo every single yearly charge later on. (Demonstrating once more that if you don't ask, you don't get.)

When all else comes up short, call and ask pleasantly. You'll be amazed by how often a courteous solicitation for help pays off.

6.  Increment credit limits.

Another factor that weighs intensely on your credit score is your credit card usage: The proportion of accessible credit to credit utilized has a significant effect. As a rule, conveying a parity of in excess of 50 percent of your affordable loan will contrarily affect your score. Maximizing your cards will hurt your score.

One approach to improve your proportion is to square away your equalizations, however another route is to expand your credit limit. If you owe $2,500 on a card with a $5,000 cutoff and you get the limit grew to $7,500, your proportion immediately improves.

To get credit limits expanded, call and ask pleasantly. If you have an excellent installment history, most credit card organizations will gladly build your breaking point - all things considered, they need you to convey a high parity. That is the manner by which they bring in cash.

Simply ensure you don't really utilize the extra accessible credit, because then you'll be back in the equivalent available credit proportion pontoon... also, you'll be more profound paying off debtors.

7.  Open another credit card account.

Another approach to expand your credit card usage proportion is to open another record. For whatever length of time that you don't convey an equalization on that card, your accessible credit quickly increments by that card's breaking point.

Attempt to get a card that doesn't charge a yearly expense, however. Your most solid option is through a bank where you as of now have a record. Without a doubt, cards with no annual payment will in general charge higher loan fees, however if you never convey an equalization, the financing cost is unessential.

8. Pay down extraordinary adjusts.

I know. You need a higher credit score because you need to acquire cash; if you had the money to square away your parities, then you won't have to obtain.

As yet: diminishing your level of accessible credit utilized can make a brisk and significant effect on your credit score. So go on a no frills financial plan to let loose money to settle your equalization. Or on the other hand sell something.

Squaring away adjusts might be hard to pull off as a transient move to expand your credit score, yet it ought to be a piece of your drawn out monetary arrangement. Not exclusively will your credit score increment after some time, you won't pay as much premium - which, if you consider it, is simply giving moneylenders cash you would prefer remained in your pocket.

9. Pay off high-intrigue, "new" credit accounts first.

Time of credit matters to your credit report. Financing costs matter to your ledger. If you have $100 every month to put toward squaring away adjusts (far beyond the necessary regularly scheduled installments, obviously), center around taking care of high intrigue accounts. Then organize those by the age of the record. Pay off the most up to date ones first; that way you'll build the normal length of credit, which should support your score, yet you'll additionally have the option to all the more rapidly abstain from paying moderately high intrigue.

Then put the cash not spent on that installment into the following record on your rundown. The "obligation snowball" framework truly accomplishes work.

10. Ride some extraordinary credit coattails (of an individual you trust.)

State your life partner has a credit card with practically zero parity and an incredible installment history; if the individual in question consents to include you as an approved client, from a credit score perspective you consequently advantage from her card's accessible credit just as her installment history.

Remember if the individual in question makes a late installment, that passage will show up as unfavorable on your credit report as well.

So pick your credit card companions carefully.

11. Keep your "old" credit cards

Your period of credit history has a moderate yet at the same time significant effect on your credit score. Let's assume you've had a specific credit card for a long time; shutting that record may diminish your general normal credit history and adversely sway your score, particularly over the present moment.

If you're planning to expand your credit score however you additionally need to dispose of a credit card account, dispose of your "most up to date" card.

12. Cover each tab on schedule.

Indeed, even one late installment can hurt your score. Do all that you can, from this day on, to consistently cover your tabs on schedule.

What's more, if one month you can't pay everything on schedule, be keen about which charges you pay late. Your home loan moneylender or credit card supplier will report a late installment to the credit departments, yet utilities and cell suppliers likely won't.

Check the "Records" segment on your credit reports to see which records are recorded, and if you need to pay late, pick a file that doesn't show up on your statement.

Then make a substantial effort to ensure you can generally pay everything on time later on. Your credit score will thank you, thus will your feelings of anxiety.

# CHAPTER 5

## INCREASE YOUR SCORE +800

N ow it is time for the hard part. Maybe you have been doing some of the work that we go through in this guidebook, and you have seen a nice increase in the amount of your FICO score. This is always good news, but now we want to take it further and see if we can get our count to 800 or higher. Only the elite have this kind of score. It is hard to get because it requires a perfect balance of types of credit, an upper credit limit, and no missed payments, among other things. But it is possible.

When you are able to get your credit to be this high, it is a lot easier for you to go through and actually get credit and loans and more any time that you would like. If a big calamity hits you and you have a bunch of medical bills to deal with, then this credit score can help you to take care of that and get your score up somewhere that will benefit you as well. or if you

would want to start a business, get a new house, or do something else along the same lines, then this high of a credit score can help you.

So, how do we ensure that we are able to get our credit score up to 800 or higher? The first thing is to know the facts. Once you are able to answer the central question of "What is a perfect credit score?" you will find that it is easier to take on the right steps in order to figure out exactly what you can do to reach the perfect score. First, though, we need to ensure we know where we stand on the FICO scale.

Once a year, you can get a free annual credit report from any of the country's top credit bureau's all three of them. If you go through this and find any issues on any of them (sometimes a mistake will show up on one and not on the others), then this is the time to fix them. You will never get to an 800+ score if there are a bunch of errors in your report.

The next thing that we can focus on is establishing a long history of credit. Most of the time, with a few exceptions, lenders are going to view borrowers with short histories of credit as riskier to work with. To reach a credit score that is 800 or higher, you have to establish, and then also maintain a long history. So even if you are not using some of the accounts, keeping them open will help you to get that score up.

As we have mentioned a bit before, you need to make sure that all of your bills are paid on time. There isn't a single person who has an 800+ credit score who also has a missed payment, or a bunch of missed payments, on their report. Paying your bills late or not paying the bills at all is going to

decrease your score. If you have trouble remembering the due dates, then consider signing up so that you can have automatic payments and have that taken care of for you.

We also need to take the time to redefine our credit card usage. About 30 percent of the score you have will consist of the utilization rate for your credit, which is going to be the amount of debt you owe divided by the total credit available. Typically, we want to stay under 30 percent, but if you are trying to get a higher score, then staying under 10 percent is best.

One thing that we have not talked about much in this guidebook yet, but will help you to get that higher score you want, is to learn how to diversify the accounts that you are holding onto. This is one of the best ways to strengthen your credit, and while this can take some to accomplish this, you will find it is a great way for us to make sure that our credit score is able to go up.

You can make your credit score stronger when you are able to diversify your accounts. This is not an excuse to go out there and open up 10 different card accounts at a time. What it means is that you should have a mix of different types of credit, such as an auto loan, a student loan, a mortgage, and a credit card. Ten credit cards are not going to be a diverse mix of debt and responsibility with your score. But having a bunch of different accounts, even if some of them have been paid off, is going to be a much better option to work with.

While you work on your credit score, you need to make sure that you can cut your spending and create a budget that you are able to stick with. This helps you to stay within means that

you can afford and makes it less likely that you are going to fall into trouble with your spending. Although it is true that your credit is not going to factor in your income, living within your means, no matter what that number is, is a great way to raise your score.

Next on the list is to find ways that you can limit the liability that you are dealing with. When you go to co-sign a loan, remember that this may seem like a beautiful thing to do, but you are really taking on a risk for another person. If you do this for someone who is not able to manage their debt all that well, it is going to negatively affect your score because you will be responsible for that debt as well. if you want to make sure that you can get a credit score that is 800+, and maintain that, then it is a good idea to avoid cosigning at all.

In addition to this one, you should make sure that your liability is limited in other manners as well. You should always report your cards that have been lost or stolen right away. If you don't do this, then it is likely that you will be liable for any of the purchases that are not authorized at the time. And if you are incapable to pay for those purchases, then your score is going to be the thing that suffers here.

And lastly, we need to make sure that we are restricting the hard inquiries that happen to our report. Whether it is you or another agency or institution who is pulling out the credit report and asking for a copy of it, you are dealing with an inquiry. A soft inquiry can happen on occasion as well, and it is generally not going to be enough to make any changes to your credit. This soft inquiry is going to happen when one of the following occurs:

1. You go through and do a check on your own credit report.

2. You give an employer you may work with in the future permission to go through and check your credit.

3. You have the financial institutions that you do business with go through and check your credit.

4. You get a credit card offer that has been preapproved, and that specific company goes through and checks your credit.

While the soft inquiry is not going to do all that much to our credit scores, we do need to be careful about the hard examination. This is going to be the one that is able to affect your credit score. It is when a company is going to pull up your credit report after you apply for a product like a credit card or a mortgage. You want to make sure that you can limit the hard inquiries as much as possible to get the best results with this.

## CHAPTER 6

# WHAT IS 609 DISPUTE LETTER AND HOW IT WORKS

## What Is 609

Basically, a 609 is known as a dispute letter, which you would send to your creditor if you saw you were overcharged or unfairly charged. Most people use a 609 message in order to get the information they feel they should have received. There are several reasons why some information might be kept from you.

A 609 letter is sent after two main steps. First, you see that the dispute is on your credit report. Second, you have already filed and processed a debt validation letter. The basis of the message is that you will use it in order to take unfair charges off of your credit report, which will then increase your credit score.

The 609 letters can quickly help you delete your bad credit. Other than this, there are a couple of other benefits you will receive from the message. One of these benefits is that you will obtain your documentation and information as the credit bureau has to release this information to you. Secondly, you will be able to get an accurate credit report, which can definitely help you increase your credit score.

There are also disadvantages to the 609 letters. One of these disadvantages is that collection agencies can add information to your credit history at any time. A second disadvantage is that you still have to repay debt. You cannot use the 609 letters in order to remove debt that you are obligated to pay. Finally, your creditor can do their own investigation and add the information back into your credit report, even if it was removed (Irby, 2019).

One of the reasons 609 came to be is because one of five people state they have inaccurate information on the credit report (Black, 2019). At the same time many people believe that this statistic is actually higher than 20 percent of Americans.

## How 609 Works To Repair Bad Credit

If you notice anything on your report that should not be there, you need to use the 609 loophole in order to file a dispute, which could result in their wrong information being taken off of the report. If this is the condition, your credit score will increase as you will no longer have this harmful inaccuracy affecting your score.

## How to File a Dispute with 609

It is important to note that there are several template letters for 609. What this means is that you can easily download and use one of these templates yourself. While you usually have to pay for them, there are some which are free. Of course, you will want to remember to include your information in the letter before you send it.

You will want to make sure everything is done correctly as this will make it more likely that the information will come off and no one will place it back on your report again.

1. Find a dispute letter through googling "609 dispute letter". While you might be able to search for a free download, for some, you will be able to copy and paste into Microsoft Word or onto a Google Doc.

2. Make the necessary changes to the letter. This will include changing the name and address. You will also want to make sure your phone number is included. Sometimes people include their email address, but this is not necessary. In fact, it is always safer to only include your home address or PO box information. You will also want to make sure to edit the whole letter. If something does not match up to what you want to say in your letter, such as what you are trying to dispute on your credit report, you need to state this. These letters are quite generic, which means you need to add in your own information.

3. You want to make sure that all of your account information you want to be taken off your credit report

is handwritten. You also want to make sure you use blue ink rather than black. On top of this, you do not need to worry about being too neat, but you want to make sure they can read the letters and numbers correctly. This is an important part of filing your dispute letter because handwritten ones in blue ink will not be pushed through their automated system. They have an automatic system which will read the letter for them and punch in the account number you use. They will then send you a generic letter that states these accounts are now off your credit report, which does not mean that it actually happened. When you write the information down, a person needs to read it and will typically take care of it. Of course, this does not mean that you will not be pushed aside. Unfortunately, this can happen with any letters.

4. You want to make sure that you prove who you are with your letters. While this is never a comfortable thing to do, you must send a copy of your social security card and your driver's license or they will shred your letter. You also need to make sure that you get each of your letters notarized. You can typically do this by visiting your county's courthouse.

5. You can send as many letters as you need to; however, keep in mind that the creditor typically will not make you send more than four. This is because when you threaten to take them to court in the third letter, they will realize that your accounts and demands just are not worth it. First, you could damage their reputation,

and secondly, you will cost them more money than simply taking the information off of your credit report will.

6. You will want to make sure that you keep all correspondence they send you. This will come in handy when they try to make you send more information or keep telling you that they cannot do anything. It is important that you do not give up. Many people struggle to get them to pay attention because that is just how the system works. Therefore, you need to make sure that you do not listen to their quick automatic reply that your information is off of your credit report. You also want to make sure to wait at least three months and then re-run your credit report to make sure the wrong information has been removed. Keep track of every time you need to re-run your credit report as you can use this as proof if they continue to send you a letter stating the information is off of your credit report.

It is important to note that you can now file a dispute letter online with all three credit bureaus. However, this is a new system, which means that it does come with more problems than sending one through the mail. While it is completely your choice whether you use a form to file your 609 dispute or send a letter, you always want to make sure you keep copies and continue to track them, even if you don't hear from the credit bureau after a couple of months. It will never hurt to send them a second letter or even a third.

# CHAPTER 7

# WHAT ARE MY RIGHTS UNDER 609?

The Fair Credit Reporting Act is going to cover a lot of the aspects and the components of credit checking to make sure that it is able to maintain a reasonable amount of privacy and accuracy along the way. This agency is going to list all of the responsibilities that credit reporting companies and any credit bureaus will have, and it also includes the rights of the consumer which will be your rights in this situation. This Act is going to be the part that will govern how everything is going to work to ensure that all parties are treated in a fair manner.

When using this act the consumer has to be told if any of the information that is on your file has been in the past or is now being used against you in any way, shape, or form. You have a right to know whether the information is harming you and what that information is.

In addition, the consumer is going to have the right to go through and dispute any information that may be seen as inaccurate or incomplete at the time. If they see that there are items in the documents they are sent, if the billing to them is not right or there is something else off in the process, the consumer has the right to dispute this and the credit reporting agency needs to at least look into it and determine if the consumer is right.

This Act is going to limit the access that third parties can have to your file. You personally have to go through and provide your consent before someone is able to go through and look at your credit score, whether it is a potential employer or another institution providing you with funding.

They are not able to get in and just look at it. Keep in mind that if you do not agree for them to take a look at the information, it is going to likely result in you not getting the funding that you want, because there are very few ways that the institution can fairly assess the risk that you pose to them in terms of creditworthiness.

it means that you may have debt or another negative item that is on your credit report, but there is a way to get around this without having to wait for years to get that to drop off your report or having to pay back a debt that you are not able to afford.

Keep in mind that this is not meant to be a method for you to take on a lot of debts that you cannot afford and then just dump them. But on occasion, there could be a few that you are able to fight and get an instant boost to your credit score in the process.

# Why Use a 609 Letter?

The 609 Letter is going to be one of the newest credit repair secrets that will help you to remove a lot of information on your credit report, all of the false information and sometimes even the accurate information, thanks to a little loophole that is found in our credit reporting laws. You can use this kind of letter in order to resolve some of the inaccuracies that show up, to dispute your errors, and handle some of the other items that could inaccurately come in and impact and lower your credit score.

Using these 609 letters is a good way for us to clean up our credit a bit and in some cases, it is going to make a perfect situation. However, we have to remember that outside of some of the obvious benefits that we are going to discuss, there are a few things that we need to be aware of ahead of time.

There are few limitations that are going to come with this as well, for example, even after you work with the 609 letters, it is possible that information that is seen as accurate could be added to the report again, even after the removal. This is going to happen if the creditor is able to verify the accuracy. They may take it off for a bit if the 30 days have passed and they are not able to verify at that point. But if the information is accurate, remember that it could end up back on the report.

# CHAPTER 8

# WHAT I NEED TO INCLUDE IN MY DISPUTE?

Writing letters to the CRAs is the most important step of the dispute process.

## Writing Dispute Letters To Furnishers

I recommended that you send a letter to the furnisher first, even though they do not have the duty to act on your letter. The letter is sent for another purpose: to provide notice of the problem so they can't later say that they were not fully informed about the nature of the dispute.

You can send the furnisher an exact copy of what you're going to send to the CRAs if the letter deals only with the furnisher's mistake. But if your CRA letter talks about multiple violations with other furnishers in the same letter, it's better that you write the furnisher a separate letter, than to send them a copy of the one you sent the CRA.

If you send the furnisher a copy of the letter you wrote to the CRA, then you should include a cover letter explaining what it is and why you're providing it. "Enclosed please find a copy of the letter I am sending to Equifax to dispute the information you provided to them."

## Technical Considerations In Writing Letters To Cras

If you want to use methods that work, then every dispute letter written must contain the following information in order to exercise your rights under the FCRA, in the event that the CRAs violate the law.

1.  Write or print your letters on paper to create an evidence trail. CRAs offer online tools to submit your disputes. Do not use these online dispute methods offered by the CRAs, for two reasons. First, you won't have a paper trail of what you did, no record of submitting your dispute. How are you going to prove they overlooked or willfully ignored their statutory duty in the absence of proof? Second, some CRAs allow you to use their online services only if you agree to waive your rights under the FCRA to file a private right of action, and agree to solve their violation of the law through binding arbitration pursuant to the Federal Arbitration Act, You do not want to waive your right to sue under the FCRA. If you have already disputed these items online, switch over immediately to writing disputes in printed or handwritten letter form from this point forward.

2.  Date the letter. This may seem like an obvious thing, but you want to keep a record of when the letter was written and sent.

3.  Mail the letters to the correct addresses.

4.  Send the Letters via Certified Mail. Do NOT send only First Class mail; otherwise, you will lose your paper trail. Send your letter only by way of certified mail through the U.S. Postal Service. There are two ways that you can send out these letters. First is Certified Mail, Return Receipt Requested. This involves attaching a green card to the back of the letter; then the Postal Service Worker hands the letter to the CRA and you are sent back through the mail a stamped or signed for green card as proof of delivery. Alternatively, you can simply send the letter "Certified Mail" without "return receipt requested." Each certified letter has a tracking number. You can go online to USPS.gov and track the delivery of the letter online. It's also cheaper not to use the return receipt requested option.

5.  Keep Physical Copies of the Letter and Proof of Delivery. Keep a copy of every letter you send. Put the Certified Letter on the letter before you send it. Keep the green card safe if you requested return receipt, and make a copy of it on 8.5 x 11 inch paper to give to an attorney later. Alternatively, PRINT OUT a copy of screenshots from the USPS website showing that the delivery was successful. Finally, keep the receipt with the tracking number when you first prepared the letter, and make a photocopy of it, too. The letter with a

tracking number, the receipt and either the return receipt or the USPS.gov website tracking printouts should all have the same certified mail receipt number.

6.  How to Send Via Certified Mail. If you do not know how to send a certified letter, check YouTube, where there are several videos people have made that will show you how to do it properly. Do a search for "USPS Tracking."

7.  Put Your Name and Address on the Letter. You need to put your name and return address on the letter so that the CRA will know where to respond to the request. I recommend putting them on the top, centered, or down by your signature at the bottom of the letter.

8.  Provide Proof of Who You Are and Where You Live. The CRAs want to make sure you are who you say you are, so they want two things to confirm this. There are two ways to do this. Sample letters provided by the FTC and CFPB merely use the Report confirmation number, date of birth, address, phone number, and "anything else they request." This may suffice but it leaves it opened ended for other requests for information, and therefore, more delays. A second way of doing this is to provide a copy of a valid, government-issued ID with your photo on it. This is usually your driver's license or state identification card if you do not drive, issued by the Department of Motor Vehicles in your state. In addition, CRAs want proof of residency. Your name on any utility bill at the address where you live is perfect. If your name is not on a utility bill, you will need to come up with something else. One other way is to send an

affidavit signed by a notary public before whom you appear in your county and state. You could use property records with your name on it, or maybe even your registration for your car. DO NOT give them your social security card OR your birth certificate. These are not necessary to comply with CRA protocols for proof of identity and residency. For furnishers (creditors or debt collectors) that you contact directly, include your account number.

9. You or Your Attorney Should Prepare and Send the Dispute Letter(s)—no one else. The FCRA states that the consumer must dispute the errors. Some attorneys who defend the CRAs in litigation argue that a dispute letter sent by someone else on behalf of the consumer, such as a Credit Repair Organization (or "CRO") does not trigger a violation because it was not sent by the consumer. Although I do not agree with the interpretation of these defense attorneys, you can avoid the issue by preparing and mailing them yourself, or hire an attorney to do it for you--someone who has legal power of attorney to act on your behalf.

## The Contents Of Your Letter To The Cras

Now that we've covered the technical aspects of writing your letters to the CRAs, let's examine what your letters should say, after you have dated the letter, added the certified mail receipt number, and used the proper address of the CRA.

Be clear and concise. Identify the problem you found on that CRA's report. "Your report states that my name is Carl." "Your

report states that I still owe Capital One $1,000." "According to your report, I have a credit card with Bank of America."

1.  Explain why that item is incorrect. "My name is Carlos, not Carl." "I do not have an outstanding balance with Capital One; I paid it off last January." "I do not have a credit card with Bank of America."

2.  Tell them what you want them to do. "Please correct the spelling of my name." "Please investigate and change the balance of the card to $0." "Please delete this reference to a Bank of America credit card."

3.  Add any additional items in your letter that you found.

4.  Attach documents in support of your claim, if you have them. "Here is a copy of my bill and the canceled check showing I paid Dr. Gruber's bill in full." You should also send back a copy of your credit report with the items circled that are in dispute. CRAs can now attach those documents when they notify furnishers that an item is in dispute, so be sure to take advantage of this. Warning: even though "e-Oscar," which is the system CRAs use to communicate with furnishers, now allows for attachments, it does not mean they will actually utilize this feature. For a complete list of all credit dispute codes used between CRAs and Furnishers, go to Appendix 6.

5.  Tell them you expect an answer in 45 days if you ordered your credit reports from AnnualCreditReport dotcom (30 days if your ordered them by phone or in writing). "Please respond to this letter within 45 days of receipt of this letter."

6. Attach proof of identity, proof of residency, and any other documents that will establish your claim.

## Do Not Do Any Of The Following:

- DO NOT use online dispute reporting methods offered by a CRA.

- DO NOT send your birth certificate.

- DO NOT use the phone to call in disputes orally.

- DO NOT send letters First Class Mail without being certified.

- DO NOT send letters without proof of identity and residency.

- DO NOT forget to keep copies of everything you send.

Many of the books that deal with letter writing contain samples that you must type up from the pages of the book. We've made the process even easier; simply go to CreditFixPower dot com and sign up as a free member. You will then have access to download sample letters in Microsoft Word form (.docx) that will make it much easier for you to prepare your letters.

# CHAPTER 9

# HOW TO WRITE A 609 CREDIT REPAIR LETTER

## Writing The Dispute Letter

Removing adverse information from your credit report is the most vital step when trying to improve your score on a short-term basis.

Credit reporting agencies (CRAs) are not obligated to give notification when adverse information is being reported about you. Upon receiving your information, the CRAs' only job under the law is to use their "reasonable procedures" to validate accuracy.

However, there is no proper and detailed explanation of these procedures, like a list of what must be performed. Of course, if the CRAs were legally required to corroborate every piece of information they receive, they will burn out and shut down.

# The Disputing Process

The first thing you need to know is that all three credit reporting agencies have to contest the inaccurate information independently. The disputed appearance may be on all three credit reports, or may not. Keep in mind that customers may not belong to all credit reporting agencies. This is why you will see that on one list some of the investors are not on the others.

Even though all three credit reporting agencies have the same information, this does not mean that if an item comes out of one credit report it will come out of the others. No promise is provided what the outcome will be. That is why you have to refute any inaccurate information about each particular article.

They can use their appeal forms when disputing with credit reporting agencies, write your own message, or challenge the item online on their Website. If you decide to dispute by letter writing, simply state the facts in a simple, concise or two sentences.

If you've found more than four entries on your credit report that you need to dispute, don't dispute everything in one letter. Whether you're writing a letter, filling out their form or answering via the Internet, break your disputes. You send or go back every 30 days to the website of the credit reporting agency, and challenge up to four more things. Don't overshoot that number. If you have to challenge less than four things, go ahead and dispute the remaining entries. Extend the spacing of conflicts for 30 days.

On submitting each address, expect to receive a revised credit report about 45 days after you send your letter or disagreement online. If your new credit report has not been issued before it's time to appeal the second time, go ahead and mail your second letter or challenge online instead.

Once all the grievance letters have been mailed or posted to their website and all the revised credit reports have been received, check whether products have been omitted or incomplete. If you need to do the procedure again for the remaining items, space 120 days from your most recent update to the next round of disputes.

## CRAs Verification Forms

The FCRA tries to balance the game for consumers with the dispute process.

The dispute process gave the CRAs so much work, so they opted to restructure their dispute process—so they designed and provided a dispute form for consumers and separate verification forms for their source creditors.

Unsurprisingly, completing and returning verification forms are easier for creditors. Moreover, because the CRAs have 30 days to answer to your dispute, either to verify or correct an item, creditors are given a few weeks to return the CRAs the verification forms. However, bear something in mind: not every source creditor will turn around these forms within the allotted period—some will not even return it, at all. Just because of this, several disputes will bring about items being corrected or deleted.

## Fill-In Dispute Forms

Below is an example of a multiple choice dispute options:

[ ] The account/item is not mine.

[ ] The account status is incorrect.

[ ] The account/item is too old to be included in my report.

When trying to initiate a dispute using the online platform, a pop-up may come to ask you if you want to dispute an item. Just select "yes" to continue.

This is just a protection clause used by the CRAs to trick you into thinking that it is illegal to dispute an item the CRAs consider as valid or correct.

Scale through their scare tactic and do not be intimidated. Just know that it is under the law for you to dispute any inaccurate information or item.

If you requested for your reports to be sent via email, among the documents will be a dispute form. The CRAs will advise to fill this already typed form only if there are any inaccuracies on your report. The funny thing is that these mailed dispute forms are simpler to complete because of two reasons:

1. Broadcasting their conformity to the legally required dispute process gives them more acclaim.

2. Supplying their forms is more convenient for them— because, with these simplified forms, their trained agents can swiftly read and convey the information on to their creditor verification forms.

If you have simple disputes (listed in a box or a line on the form), you can either use the online or mailed disputes forms. However, if your issues are complex or lengthy and cannot fit into the allotted space or there are not enough options on the document to address all your dispute issues, you may need to write the CRAs.

Concerning the mailed fill-in dispute forms, be cautious when filling them out as they may ask you to give out more personal information to the CRAs than you need to. The CRAs asking for more information does not mean you have to provide it. Just remember that if a fill-in dispute form does not adequately help your case, the best course of action is to write your letter.

## How To Write Your Own Dispute Letter

After organizing all your items, you can write your letter, but make sure to put your disputes in one correspondence. It does not matter if you have a long list of disputes. You can arrange your disputes on multiple pages and in different ways.

For instance, in the left column, list all your accounts; in the right column, list the issues in a few words ("not my account," "always paid on time/never late," etc.). Alternatively, you explain your dispute first, then list the accounts associated with the issue. For example, "the following accounts do not belong to me. . ." Just keep it short and straightforward.

When disputing an item with the bureaus you want to be sure that you have a valid reason and are requesting the correct items to be investigated.

Making sure that you are air tight in your dispute reasoning is important.

You will find that dispute reasons will add validity to your future disputes. If you choose to hire an attorney to pursue legal actions, the letters submitted may be called to be used in court.

Do yourself a favor and make sure you are using real dispute instructions with real reasoning behind them. What is meant by this is that you want to make sure that if you are disputing an account and you do not have solid proof that it is reporting inaccurately or in error then leave some room to be wrong. If you come out and say - THIS ACCOUNT ISN'T MINE, then you is lying and are committing fraud (don't do that).

## Sending Your Dispute Letter

When correcting information on your credit report, make sure it reflects with all three CRAs. Even when one or two reports do not show an error appearing on the other, be on the safe side by telling all of them about the error. Do it because the error might be a recent one and has yet to spread to other reports.

Even if you have not received all three reports, send a dispute letter to all three CRAs. Know that you are a consumer, so an error on one report could mean the same error is on other reports. It is not crime disputing with all CRAs. Of course, if you can start the dispute process with one CRA, you will not have much trouble doing with the others. When a CRA cannot find an error, it will respond with a letter informing you about it.

Whether you are using the CRA dispute form or drafting your dispute letter, use only certified mail with return receipt requested. While a CRA hardly claims not to have received your letter, sending certified mail is still best for your correspondence, especially in cases of pressing legal disputes like identity theft.

Call the CRA to know whether your dispute was received. Note that when talking with CRA agents, be careful not to give them the information you do not want to be included on your report.

The following is a list of CRA customer service phone numbers:

- Equifax: (800) 685-1111

- Experian: (888) 397-3742

- TransUnion: (800) 916-8800

As soon as a CRA gets your dispute letter, it notifies you, and then informs you later of the completion of the verification process. You may get a response much sooner than 30 days— it all depends on the number of accounts you are disputing and the speed of at which source creditors give back the verification forms. Still, give it up to 40 days. If you do not get anything after 40 days, know that your dispute was not recognized, so send another one.

# What Is Found In A CRA's Response To A Dispute?

After receiving your corrected reports, carefully read through them. The first or second page should include a paragraph stating the information reinvestigated upon your request, next is a list of affected accounts and the results of the reinvestigation. Here you will see one or more of the three possible outcomes regarding the dispute process:

1. Deleted: Deleted accounts—like they never existed.

2. Verified—No Change: No changes were made. The accounts will continue to report information

3. Update: This could mean one of three things:

I. Deleted late or past due indications.

II. After the review of the account by the source creditor, a small adjustment was made, and it does not affect your report.

III. Along with the forms, the source creditor returns an updated submission on your file (a requirement after every few months) to update your account. In this case, do not be fooled by the "update" notification, and make sure the first issue has been addressed. If not, send a follow-up letter.

## Make Sure Everything Is Readable

No matter what you send, you want to make sure that someone else will be able to read it. This is another reason why having someone proofread your letter is often the best option as they will be able to tell you if something isn't readable or doesn't make sense.

While you should do your best to type as much information as possible, you shouldn't write the letter by hand. While this will be accepted, it is generally not something that people do in this day and age. Furthermore, typing most of the information will ensure that words are not mistaken for another word, which can happen with handwriting. While you might feel your handwriting is easily readable, someone else might not be able to understand it as well.

# CHAPTER 10

# 609 CREDIT REPAIR LETTER TEMPLATES

## Letter #1

(Initial Letter To Credit Bureau Disputing Items)

{Name of Bureau}

{Address}

{Date}

{Name on account}

{Report number}

To whom it may concern:

On {Date of Credit Report} I received a copy of my credit report which contains errors that are damaging to my credit score. I am requesting the following items be completely investigated as each account contains several mistakes.

{Creditor 1 / Account number}

{Creditor 2 / Account number}

{Creditor 3 / Account number}

Thank you in advance for your time. I understand that you need to check with the original creditors on these accounts and that you will make sure every detail is accurate. I also understand that under the Fair Credit Reporting Act you will need to complete your investigation within 30 days of receiving this letter. Once you are finished with your investigation, please send me a copy of my new credit report showing the changes. Looking forward to hear from you as I am actively looking for a new job and wouldn't want these mistakes on my credit report to stand in my way.

Sincerely,

{Your signature}

{Your Printed Name}

{Your Address}

{Your Phone Number}

{Your Social Security Number}

**Attach a copy of the credit report showing which accounts you are disputing**

# Letter #2

(When you don't get a response from Letter #1)

{Name of Bureau}

{Address}

{Date}

{Name on account}

{Report number}

To whom it may concern:

On {Date of your first letter} I sent you a letter asking you to investigate several mistakes on my credit report. I've included a copy of my first letter and a copy of the report with the mistakes circled. The Fair Credit Reporting Act says I should only have to wait 30 days for the investigation to be finished. It has been more than 30 days and I still have not heard anything.

I'm guessing that since you have not responded that you were not able to verify the information on the mistaken accounts. Since it has been more than 30 days, please remove the mistakes from my credit report and send me a copy of my updated credit report. Also, as required by law, please send an updated copy of my credit report to anyone who requested a copy of my credit file in the past six months.

Looking forward to hear from you as I am actively looking for a new job and wouldn't want these mistakes on my credit report to stand in my way.

Sincerely,

{Your signature}

{Your Printed Name}

{Your Address}

{Your Phone Number}

{Your Social Security Number}

**Attach a copy of the credit report showing which accounts you are disputing**

**Attach a copy of your original letter**

**Attach a copy of the registered letter receipts showing the date they received your original letter**

# Letter #3

(Request for removal of negative items from original creditor)

{Name of Creditor}

{Address}

{Date}

{Name on account}

To whom it may concern:

On {Date of Credit Report} I received a copy of my credit report which contains errors that are damaging to my credit score. I am requesting the following items be completely investigated as each account contains several mistakes.

{Description of item(s) you are disputing/account number(s)}

I have enclosed a duplicate of the credit report and have highlighted the account(s) in question.

Thank you in advance for your time. I understand that you need to check on these accounts and that you will make sure every detail is accurate. I also understand that under the Fair Credit Reporting Act you will need to complete your investigation within 30 days of receiving this letter. Once you are finished with your investigation, please alert all major credit bureaus where you have reported my information. Also, please send me a letter confirming the changes.

Looking forward to hear from you as I am actively looking for a new job and wouldn't want these mistakes on my credit report to stand in my way.

Sincerely,

{Your signature}

{Your Printed Name}

{Your Address}

{Your Phone Number}

{Your Social Security Number}

**Attach a copy of the credit report showing which accounts you are disputing**

# Letter #4

(If you don't receive a response from Letter #3)

{Name of Creditor}

{Address}

{Date}

{Name on account}

To whom it may concern:

On {Date of your first letter} I sent you a letter asking you to investigate several mistakes on my credit report. I've included a copy of my first letter and a copy of the report with the mistakes circled. The Fair Credit Reporting Act says I should only have to wait 30 days for the investigation to be finished. It has been more than 30 days and I still have not heard anything.

I'm guessing that since you have not responded that you were not able to verify the information on the mistaken accounts. Since it has been more than 30 days, please immediately report the updated information to all major credit bureaus so they may update my credit report. Also, please send me a letter confirming these changes to the way you report my account.

Looking forward to hear from you as I am actively looking for a new job and wouldn't want these mistakes on my credit report to stand in my way.

Sincerely,

{Your signature}

{Your Printed Name}

{Your Address}

{Your Phone Number}

{Your Social Security Number}

**Attach a copy of the credit report showing which accounts you are disputing**

**Attach a copy of your original letter**

**Attach a copy of the registered letter receipts showing the date they received your original letter**

# Letter #5

(If the Credit Bureau doesn't remove negative items disputed)

{Name of Credit Bureau}

{Address}

{Date}

{Name on account}

{Report number}

To whom it may concern:

On {Date of your first letter} I sent you a letter asking you to investigate several mistakes on my credit report. I've included a copy of my first letter and a copy of the report with the mistakes circled. According to your response you have chosen to leave these negative items on my credit report adding insult to injury. The items in question are:

{Creditor 1 / Account number}

{Creditor 2 / Account number}

{Creditor 3 / Account number}

I find it completely unacceptable that you and the creditor refuse to investigate my dispute properly. Your refusal to follow the Fair Credit Reporting Act is causing me untold stress and anxiety. Since you won't follow through, I want to know exactly how you investigated each account. Therefore, I would like the name, title and contact information for the person at the creditor with whom you did the investigation. This will let me personally follow up with the creditor and find out why they are choosing to report these mistakes on my

credit month after month.

I see I am only one person among thousands or more that you have to look after, but to me this is both personally damaging and humiliating. You may not understand it and you don't have to--all I'm asking is that when people look at my credit file, they see the most accurate information and that's not what's happening.

Please provide me with the requested information right away so I can finally put this nightmare behind me.

Looking forward to hear from you as I am actively looking for a new job and wouldn't want these mistakes on my credit report to stand in my way.

Sincerely,

{Your signature}

{Your Printed Name}

{Your Address}

{Your Phone Number}

{Your Social Security Number}

**Attach a copy of the credit report showing which accounts you are disputing**

**Attach a copy of your original letter**

**Attach a copy of the Bureau's response showing no changes to your credit**

# CHAPTER 11

## 609 CREDIT REPAIR LETTER TEMPLATES PART 2

### Letter 6:
### Affidavit Of Unknown Inquiries

EQUIFAX

P.O. box 740256

ATLANTA GA 30374

My name Is John William; my current address is 6767. W Phillips Road, San Jose, CA 78536, SSN: 454-02-9928, Phone: 415-982-3426, Birthdate: 6-5-1981

I checked my credit reports and noticed some inquiries from companies that I did not give consent to access my credit reports; I am very concerned about all activity going on with my credit reports these days. I immediately demand the removal of these inquiries to avoid any confusion as I DID NOT initiate these inquires or give any form of consent

electronically, in person, or over the phone. I am fully aware that without permissible purpose no entity is allowed to pull my credit unless otherwise noted in section 604 of the FCRA.

The following companies did not have permission to request my credit report:

CUDL/FIRST CALIFORNIA ON 6-15-2017
CUDL/NASA FEDERAL CREDIT UNION ON 6-15-2017
LOANME INC 3-14-2016
CBNA on 12-22-2017

I once again demand the removal of these unauthorized inquiries immediately.

THANK YOU

(Signature)

# Letter 7:
# Affidavit Of Suspicious Addresses

1-30-2018

ASHLEY WHITE
2221 N ORANGE AVE APT 199
FRESNO CA 93727
PHONE: 559-312-0997
SSN: 555-59-4444
BIRTHDATE: 4-20-1979

EQUIFAX
P.O. box 740256
ATLANTA GA 30374

To whom it may concern:

I recently checked a copy of my credit report and noticed some addresses reporting that do not belong to me or have been obsolete for an extended period of time. For the safety of my information, I hereby request that the following obsolete addresses be deleted from my credit reports immediately;

4488 N white Ave apt 840 Fresno, CA 93722
4444 W Brown Ave apt 1027 Fresno CA 93722
13330 E Blue Ave Apt 189 Fresno CA 93706

I have provided my identification card and social security card to verify my identity and current address. Please notify any creditors who may be reporting any unauthorized past accounts that are in connection with these mentioned addresses as I have exhausted all of my options with the furnishers.

 (Your signature)

***This letter is to get a response from the courts to show the credit bureaus that you have evidence that they cannot legally validate the Bankruptcy***

# Letter 8:
# Affidavit Of James Robert

U.S BANKRUPTCY COURT

700 STEWART STREET 6301

SEATTLE, WA 98101

RE: BANKRUPTCY (164444423TWD SEATTLE, WA)

To whom it may concern:

My Name is JAMES ROBERT my mailing address is 9631 s 2099h CT Kent, WA 99999.

I recently reviewed my credit reports and came upon the above referenced public record. The credit agencies have been contacted and they report in their investigation that you furnished or reported to them that the above matter belongs to me. This act may have violated federal and Washington state privacy laws by submitting such information directly to the credit agencies, Experian, Equifax, and Transunion via mail, phone or fax.

I wish to know if your office violated Washington State and federal privacy laws by providing information on the above referenced matter via phone, fax or mail to Equifax, Experian or TransUnion.

Please respond as I have included a self-addressed envelope,

Thank You

(your signature)

# Letter 9:
# Affidavit Of Erroneous Entry

***Dispute letter for bankruptcy to credit bureaus***

1-1-18

JAMES LEE
131 S 208TH CT
KENT WA 98031
SSN: 655-88-0000
PHONE: 516-637-5659
BIRTHDATE: 10-29-1985

EXPERIAN
P. O. Box 4500
Allen, TX 75013

RE: BANKRUPTCY (132323993TWD SEATTLE, WA)

To whom it may concern:

My Name is James LEE my mailing address is 131 s 208th CT Kent, WA 98031

I recently disputed the entry of a bankruptcy that shows on my credit report which concluded as a verified entry your bureau. I hereby request your methods of verification, if my request cannot be met, I demand that you delete this entry right away and submit me an updated credit report showing the changes.

Thank You

(Your signature)

# Letter10:
# Affidavit For Account Validation

***First letter you send to the credit bureaus for disputes***

1-18-2019

TRANSUNION
P.O. BOX 2000
CHESTER PA 19016

To Whom It May Concern:

My name is John Doe, SSN: 234-76-8989, my current address is 4534. N Folk street Victorville, CA 67378, Phone: 310-672-0929 and I was born on 4-22-1988.

After checking my credit report, I have found a few accounts listed above that I do not recognize. I understand that before any account or information can be furnished to the credit bureaus; all information and all accounts must be 100% accurate, verifiable and properly validated. I am not disputing the existence of this debt, but I am denying that I am the responsible debtor. I am also aware that mistakes happen, I believe these accounts can belong to someone else with a similar name or with my information used without my consent either from the furnisher itself or an individual.

I am demanding physical documents with my signature or any legally binding instruments that can prove my connection to these erroneous entries, Failure to fully verify that these accounts are accurate is a violation of the FCRA and must be removed or it will continue to damage my ability to obtain additional credit from this point forward.

I hereby demand that the accounts listed above be legally validated or be removed from my credit report immediately.

Thank You

(Your signature)

## Letter 11:
## Affidavit Of Request For Method Verification

***Second letter to Credit Bureau if they verified anything***

10-22-17

JOSHUA ETHAN
2424 E Dawn Hill way
Merced, CA 93245
SSN: 555-22-3333
Phone: 415-222-9090
Birthdate: 9-29-1987

EQUIFAX
P.O. BOX 740256
ATLANTA GA 30374

To whom it may concern:

I recently submitted a request for investigation on the following accounts which were determined as verified:

Acct Numbers# (XXXXXXX COLLECTION AGENCY A)
(XXXXXXX COLLECTION AGENCY B)

I submitted enough information for you to carry out a reasonable investigation of my dispute, you did not investigate this account or account(s) thoroughly enough as you chose to verify the disputed items.

Under section 611 of the FCRA I hereby request the methods in which you verified these entries. If you cannot provide me with a reasonable reinvestigation and the methods of which you used for verification, please delete these erroneous entries from my credit report. Furthermore, I would like to be presented with all relevant documents pertaining to the disputed entries.

I look forward to resolving this manner

(Your signature)

# Letter 12:
# Affidavit For Validation

***This is the first letter sent to the collection agency if the account is already on your credit reports***

1-22-2017

JAMES DANIEL
13233 ROYAL LANDS
LAS VEGAS NV 89141
SSN: 600-60-0003
BIRTHDATE: 2-18-1991
PHONE: 702-331-3912

EXPERIAN
P. O. BOX 4500
ALLEN, TX 75013

To Whom It May Concern:

After reviewing my credit reports, I noticed this unknown item that you must have furnished in error, I formally deny being responsible for any parts of this debt.

Please send me any and all copies of the original documentation that legally binds me to this account, also including the true ownership of this debt.

This account is unknown to me and I formally ask that your entity cease all reporting of this account to the credit agencies and cease all collection attempts.

ACCOUNT: UNIVERSITY OF PHOENIX (IRN 9042029892)

If you cannot present what I request, I demand you stop reporting this account to the credit bureaus to avoid FCRA and

FDCPA violations and cease all contact efforts and debt collection activity.

Please respond in writing within 30 days so we can resolve this matter without any more violations.

Thank you.

(Your signature)

# Letter 13:
# Affidavit Of Method Verification

***Second letter to collection agency if they verified anything***

1-30-2018

JAMES DAVID
1111 N FAIR AVE APT 101
FRESNO CA 93706
PHONE: 559-399-0999
SSN: 555-59-5599
BIRTHDATE: 9-25-1979

EXPERIAN
P. O. BOX 4500
ALLEN, TX 75013

To Whom It May Concern:

I previously disputed this account with your company and it resulted in you verifying this entry. I am once again demanding validation of this debt for the second time as I have yet to receive sufficient documentation that legally shows I am responsible for this matter.

In addition to requesting validation, I am formally requesting your method of verification for these entries that I have previously disputed, please supply me with any documentation you may have on file to aid your stance.

If this entry cannot be validated or if the method of verification cannot be provided to me in a timely manner, I demand that you delete this entry immediately.

Thank you.

(Your signature)

# Letter 14:
# Affidavit Of Fraudulent Information

***Letter to Credit Bureau for identity theft***

10-17-17

HELEN JOHNSON
2525 S CHERRY AVE APT 201
FRESNO, CA 93702
PHONE 559-299-2328
BIRTHDAY 11-30-1990
SOCIAL SECURITY NUMBER 555-89-1111

EQUIFAX CONSUMER
FRAUD DIVISION
P.O. BOX 740256
ATLANTA GA 30374

To whom it may concern:

I am writing this letter to document all of the accounts reported by these furnishers that stem from identity theft. I have read and understand every right I have under section 605B and section 609 of the FCRA. Please block the following accounts that are crippling my consumer reports as I do not recognize, nor am I responsible for, nor have I received any money or goods from the creation of these unknown accounts.

Please refer to Police Report and ID Theft Affidavit attached.

1) CBE GROUP (12323239XXXX)
2) LOBEL FINANCIAL (431XXXX)

Please contact each credit to prevent further charges, activity, or authorizations of any sort regarding my personal information.

Thank you

(Your signature)

# Letter 15:
# Affidavit of fraudulent information

***Letter to lender or collection agency when reporting fraudulent accounts***

10-15-17

TARA BROWN
3421 N ROSE AVE APT 211
OAKLAND CA 93766
PHONE 559-369-9999
BIRTHDAY 9-20-1979
SOCIAL SECURITY NUMBER 584-00-0222
MONTGOMERY WARD

RE Account # 722222XXXX

TRANSUNION
P.O. BOX 2000
CHESTER PA 19016

To whom it may concern:

I have recently reviewed my credit reports and found an account listed that I do not recognize. I am informing you today that you are reporting the above-mentioned account that is a result of identity theft, and continuing to report this entry will be in violation under FACTA rules and regulations.

I have never had this account MONTGOMERY WARD 99986518XXXX, I ask that you to cease all reporting and collection activity surrounding this account which is my right under section 605B of the FCRA, please refer to police report.

I ask that this information be blocked and disregarded from your accounting. Thank you for your time and I will be eagerly waiting for your response.

Thank You

(Your signature)

# CHAPTER 12

# CEASE AND DESIST AND GOODWILL LETTERS

## Cease and Desist Letters

The reasons that you might want to send a cease and desist letter and the pros and cons of doing so were explained. You want to include your contact information and the account number that you want to stop being contacted about. Use this as a last resort for stopping collection companies as it can backfire, leading to your case being brought to court. Writing a cease and desist letter is quite different from writing a dispute letter. Pay attention to their differences.

To make a cease and desist letter you should:

- Use professional yet firm language.

- Reference the Fair Debt Collections Practice Act (FDCPA).

- Keep all original copies for your records.

- Send your letter via certified mail.

To make a cease and desist letter you should not:

- Incriminate yourself in anything that the collection agency might have accused you of doing.
- Use personal language.

## Cease and Desist Letter Template

Date

Your Name
Your Address
Your City, State, Zip Code

Name of Collection Agency
Address
City, State, Zip Code

Re: Account Number

To [ Name of Collection Agency],

Under Fair Debt Collections Practices Act (FDCPA), Public laws 95 – 109 and 99 – 361, I am formally notifying you to cease all communications with me regarding my debt for this account and any other debts that you have purported that I owe.

I will file an objection with the Federal Trade Commission and the [Your State] Attorney General's office as well as pursue criminal and civil claims against you and your company if you attempt to continue contacting me after you receive this notice. If I receive any further communications after you have confirmed receipt of this notice, the communications may be recorded as evidence for my claims against you.

You should also be aware that any negative information related to this account on my credit reports will be handled with all legal rights available to me.

Regards,

Your Name

Signature

## Goodwill Letters

Goodwill letters are not a guaranteed method of removing negative information from your credit report but are still worth a try in some situations. They are more effective if you have a good history with the company, have had a technical error delayed your payment, or if your autopay did not go through. You can sometimes even convince a credit company to forgive a late payment if you simply forgot to pay.

Try to contact your credit agency by phone to negotiate and explain your situation before sending a goodwill letter. This tactic might be all that you need to do in order to remove the record of the late payment. The sooner you contact, the better as well. If you notice that you have a late payment, calling right away could stop it from being reported at all.

To write a goodwill letter you should:

- Use courteous language that reflects your remorse for the late payment and thank the company for their service.
- Include reasons you need to have the record removed such as qualifying for a home or auto loan or insurance.

- Accept that you were at fault for the late payment.

- Explain what caused the payment to be made late.

To write a goodwill letter you should not:

- Be forceful, rude, or flippant about the situation.

## Goodwill Letter Template

Date

Your Name
Your Address
Your City, State, Zip Code

Name of Credit Company
Address
City, State, Zip Code

Re: Account Number

Dear Sir or Madam,

Thank you [company's name] for continued service. I am writing in regard to an urgent request concerning a tradeline on my credit reports that I would like to have reconsidered. I have taken pride in making my payments on time and in full since I received [name of credit line/card] on [date that you received the credit]. Unfortunately, I was unable to pay on time [date of missed payment(s)] due to [detailed and personal reasons for not being able to pay on time. You might want to include several sentences using as much information as possible to plead your case.]

[Follow up your reason for not paying on time with a concession of guilt such as:] I have come to see that despite

[reason listed above], I should have been better prepared/ more responsible with my finances to ensure the payment was on time. I have worked on [some type of learning or way of improving your situation] in order to prevent this situation from happening again.

I am in need of/about to apply for [new credit line such as a home loan] and it has come to my attention that the notation on my credit report of [credit company's] late payment may prevent me from qualifying or receiving the best interest rates. Due to the fact that this notation is not a reflection of my status with [credit company], I am requesting that you please give me another chance at a positive credit rating by revising my tradelines.

If you need any additional documentation or information from me in order to reach a positive outcome, please feel free to contact me.

Thank you again for your time,

Sincerely yours,

Your Name

Signature

# CHAPTER 13

# ELIMINATE HARMFUL ERRORS AND INACCURACIES

You need to eliminate all harmful credit report errors and inaccuracies from all three credit bureaus. The U.S. Public Interest Research Group (PIRG), an advocacy group, released a survey indicating that seven out of every ten credit reports contained some kind of error or mistake. The survey also found one out of every four credit reports had errors considered serious enough to prevent a borrower from getting a loan or credit. This survey shows we need to make sure our credit report is accurate actively. You are working hard to build your credit, do not allow other people's errors to affect you negatively. ...To hinder your hard work and earned rewards.

Every credit report is built on information gathered, purchased, and reported by creditors and third party groups. If false or inaccurate information has made it to your credit

report, then your credit report will reflect this false or inaccurate information.  False or inaccurate information in your credit report can harm your credit and cause you to pay more in interest rate, credit fees, loan costs, or even prevent you from getting loans.

The sooner you identify harmful errors or inaccuracies in your credit report and work with your creditor and credit bureau to correct them, the sooner your credit score will improve. However, not all errors and inaccuracies are harmful.

Credit Scenario:  A revolving credit account (such as a credit card) was opened over 12 months ago, the credit limit is $1,000.00 dollars, the balance owed is three hundred dollars or less, and all monthly payments have been made on time.

Not Harmful: Any increase to your credit history or your credit limit only helps your credit and should not be corrected.

Harmful: Any decrease made to your credit history, either to your credit limit or the report of any late payments, are harmful and should be corrected as soon as possible

- Credit experts recommend individuals review their credit reports at least once every 12 months for harmful inaccuracies and errors. Data on how to order free credit reports are found below.

- It is important to verify the accuracy of dates, especially on every negative credit report.  Bankruptcy, foreclosures, repossessions, late payments and other negative credit information begin losing their negative effect after twelve months. Reviewing your credit report for accurate dates allows you to get rid of past negative

events sooner.

- Check for indications you have been a victim of identity fraud. Search your report for names, social security numbers, and accounts that are not yours.

Note: Some creditors "re-age" debt. This means a creditor may report negative information like a bankruptcy, foreclosure, judgment or collections as recently as today, as opposed to the true date. Re-aging is done for many reasons, from a simple reporting error to full manipulation by the creditor with the purpose of selling the "fresh debt" to debt collectors. Re-aging negative reports is something you need to be on the lookout for because it will significantly hurt your credit. If you find negative information has been re-aged, immediately work with that creditor and credit bureau to correct the error.

## Credit Report Errors:

The credit report is the key to building and improving your credit score. The quicker you build credit and show a strong twelve months of credit history, the quicker you can improve your credit score. However, excessive credit use, late or non-payments, and errors all hurt your credit score.

A credit report error can be as simple as having repeated or duplicated collection account, wrong address or wrong account name. Credit report errors can include reduced or missing credit limits, inflated credit balances, debts belonging to other people, multiple social security numbers, wrong addresses, and wrong or incorrect variations on your name.

Simply speaking, you can combine most credit errors into two groups: high priority and low priority credit errors.  Since all credit scores are based solely on the credit report, removing high priority errors will result in the quickest and most permanent improvements.

High priority credit errors include inaccurate reporting of credit limits and balances owed.  In order to build and strengthen your credit, it is important to show as high a credit limit as possible, with a balanced owed of no more than 30% of the credit limit.  Other high priority credit errors include an old bankruptcy being reported as filed within the last year.

Low priority credit errors include inaccurate reporting of irrelevant or helpful factors.  Exaggerated credit limits will not hurt you.  A repossession of an auto ten years ago, being reported as occurring eight years ago will not hurt your credit.  Do not correct errors that are in your favor.  Low priority credit errors are not likely hurting your credit score and can be ignored.  Focus your time and resources on correcting high priority negative errors.

## High-Priority Credit Report Errors:

- Collection notices listed more than once (duplicates)
- Mistakes or errors in your payment history that occurred within the past two years
- Missing or reduced account credit limits
- Collection notices that are not yours
- Incorrect information such as current address, previous addresses, and current employer

- Accounts that do not belong to you (this could indicate identity fraud or the beginning of your credit report being merged with another person's report)

- Someone else's Social Security number or a mistake in your Social Security number (this could indicate identity fraud or the beginning of your credit report being merged with another person's report)

- Someone else's name or a mistake in your name (this could indicate identity fraud or the beginning of your credit report being merged with another person's report)

## Low-Priority Credit Report Errors:

- Mistakes in your payment history that occurred more than two years ago

- Delinquencies older than seven years

- Beneficial account inaccuracies (e.g. inflated credit limits)

- Wrong date of birth is a low priority error — unless you think you might be a victim of identity fraud

- Typos in account numbers are low priority — unless you believe you might be a victim of identity fraud

## Disputing Credit Report Errors:

If after reviewing each credit report you find a high priority credit error — what's next? You need to take action and get those errors deleted or corrected as quickly as possible. Begin by writing the offending credit bureau and the creditor directly. See the Appendix called "credit dispute letter" for an

example of a dispute letter and the Appendix called "how to get your free credit report" and "identity theft: how to report it" for credit bureau contact information. Be sure your letter specifies the error and be specific in how the error needs to be corrected, and request a letter confirming the action taken be mailed to you.

Disputing an error with a credit bureau or creditor is free. Once you formally contact them, they will investigate the disputed claim and, if applicable, delete or correct the error. The following three steps are recommended when disputing an error with the credit bureaus.

## Step one:  Contact the offending credit bureau

- It is possible that not all creditors report to all the credit bureaus.  For this reason, only contact the credit bureau(s) that is reporting the erroneous negative credit information.

- Use the "credit report dispute letter--sample" found in the appendix.

- Explain in your letter what is inaccurate and give specific directions as to the corrective action you want taken.

- When possible, include proof in your letter to support the claim.

- Enclose a copy of the credit report, with the item(s) in question circled.  (Make sure to send the credit report to the corresponding credit bureau.)

- Within 30 days, the credit bureau is supposed to confirm with the creditor and investigate the disputed information.

- The creditor is required by law to investigate the disputed data and report its findings.

- If the dispute results in a change to your credit report, the credit bureau will send you a written response and a free copy of your updated credit report.

- However, if the creditor disagrees with your claim, the credit bureau will mail you a written explanation stating the disputed item is accurate.

## Step two:  Keep a record

- Keep records of all phone and email communications.

- Keep copies of every letter sent and received.

- Keep proof supporting your claim — this can include anything from canceled payment checks to past billing statements.

- If you're missing key billing statements, the Fair Credit Billing Act requires each creditor keep past statements on file which you can request for a fee.

- Call the creditors billing or record's department and ask for what you need.

## Step three:  Keep at it

Continue to check your credit reports at least once every 12 months.  Make sure no new derogatory or harmful errors or negative information has been added to your credit report, and the corrected errors have not been included in your credit record.

Note:  You are not alone in this fight.  As of 2012, you can now ask the federal government to help you fix credit report errors.

# CHAPTER 14

## HOW IMPORTANT IS THE FICO SCORE?

Though there are different scoring models outside of the FICO score, 90 percent of lenders will use the FICO score as an evaluation of creditworthiness. When most people think about the FICO score, they think about one score or one calculation being used. There are six varieties in the FICO system lenders commonly use:

1. The Generic FICO Score

2. The FICO Mortgage Industry Option Score

3. The Auto Industry Option Score

4. The FICO Bankcard Score

5. The FICO Installment Loan Score

6. The FICO Personal Finance Score

The basic FICO formula is still intact even with these different varieties, but the emphasis is they are industry specific. To keep it simple, there is the base version, such as the FICO 08, and the industry-specific versions like the Mortgage Industry Option Score. The best place to check the specific version to your lending needs to visit MYFICO dotcom.

My intent is not to complicate the process or confuse you; I'm simply shedding light on the possibility that lenders are using a score far different from the ones you receive from most consumer credit reporting websites.

There is even a score specific to the insurance industry called the credit-based insurance score. This score is used to predict the likelihood of a consumer not paying premiums on-time and the actual premium payments itself. Insurance companies also utilize this score to determine if an applicant will be accepted or denied for insurability. Imagine that when you consider all the various types of insurance we actually use. At the end of the day, it's all about a calculation of risk.

In order to understand the financial downturn, credit reports and legal debt dumping, some historical backgroundon how these companies all work illegally should be considered. Search for terms such as: "the gig is up," and "money the Federal Reserve and you" to get the real deal on how money works and how you've been cheated for your whole life!

You're getting there now! You know we have fake money so collectors can never take money from you because none was loaned. Search the term "FTC debt video" to see how easy it is to record those collection calls and get free money when collectors start talking funny. Another search term like "man

wins $1.5 million from collector"shows how you can even do it accidentally!

In case you didn't get rich by recording the phone calls,you can still dump the debt by answering those collectionnotices with the demand for a proof of debt letter. Doesn't get much simpler than that does it? The plastic is gone,so let's do the 850 FICO score stuff.

By now, you've probably figured out every thing is totallyopposite from what you thought. The same thing is trueof the credit reporting industry. According to section 609of the Fair Credit Reporting Act, they must have verifiable proof that what they're reporting is true. You don't begthem to correct some inaccuracy. You tell them to show you verifiable proof or take it off your report.

Time to celebrate your new knowledge base so throw a little Orville Redenbacher's Pop Secret in the nuke and think about this: you don't need a credit report to dump the cards. Make a fortune off the collector while you're dumping the debt, get a free credit report, then jump on the reporting agencies and tell them to take anything you want off your credit history.

How often do you check your report?

Checking your credit report is vital when it comes to preparing your financial future. Online resources make it easier than ever for you to review your report, and checking it is free. But how do you know when and how often you need to review your report? If you are preparing for a financed or majorpurchase, you will want to review your report prior to applying for a loan or line of credit.

The interest rate you pay on a mortgage loan, auto loanand your credit card interest rates all are determined by your credit score. Keep in mind that three out of four credit reportscontain errors. Those mistakes could be negatively affectingyour credit score without your knowledge. Review yourreport closely and keep an eye out for any inaccurate or repetitive information.

By law, the credit reporting agencies must remove any errors that appear on your report, but it can take 30 days or more to do so. If you know you have a financed purchase in your near future, be sure to review your report immediately so you have ample time to correct any errors before it affects your loan.

If you are in the process of purchasing a home, you will also want to monitor your report closely. Even if you have secured a mortgage commitment from the bank, you will still need to keep a watchful eye on your credit report. Banks do a last minute credit check prior to the closing. Problems with your credit report could jeopardize your home purchase, so be sure to periodically check your report until you close on your new home.

Even if you do not plan to make any major purchases, checking your report periodically can alert you to any issues or potential identity theft. It is a good policy to review your reportquarterly to ensure that your finances are on the right track.

When applying for mortgage financing, your credit score is going to be one of the first things a potential lender looks at. Especially these days when lenders are tightening lending requirements; a good score can be especially important.

Credit scores are used by mortgage lenders to determine your level of financial responsibility. A low credit score may indicate that you might be a bad credit risk, which could mean that you might default on your mortgage loan.

Of course, other factors are also taken into consideration when applying for a mortgage loan, such as a person's income and employment status. However, the credit score can often be the deciding factor. Even if you are approved for a mortgage loan with less than perfect credit, there will be a price to be paid. This is because only individuals who have good credit ratings will qualify for the best interest rates.

# CHAPTER 15

## HOW YOUR SCORE IS GENERATED?

**E**very time you apply for credit your records are stored and used to build towards a credit profile. Whether you've taken out a mortgage, personal loan, credit card, overdraft, contract mobile phone, utility bills or even monthly car insurance, your details will be checked and added to in order to predict how likely you are to cause risk.

Missing bill payments or making late payments can have a negative affect on your score, which may lead to future credit applications being rejected.

Lenders use several pieces of information when deciding whether you pass their acceptance criteria, including data held by three credit reference agencies - Experian, Equifax and Callcredit.

If you have no previous experience with credit, it is unlikely that you have a credit history. This can work against you want to borrow, as lenders prefer to have some kind of reassurance that you can be trusted to pay back the money owed, which usually gained from looking at your previous track record.

## Building A Good Score

There are several ways in which you can both improve or repair your credit score, so if you have poor, adverse or no credit history at all then help is at hand. While there is no an exact science to improving your score, there are several things you can do to sway lenders' attitudes towards you.

If you haven't done so already, open a bank account and/or savings account. This may not be so simple if you don't have a respectable credit score, so you may have to look at a guaranteed bank account, although these bank accounts come with limited features, for example you may not be given access to a debit card.

Apply for and make use of Credit cards. While this doesn't always appear to be the best advice, it is very important in your quest to build up a good score. The golden rule which will earn you a good score is to ALWAYS pay at least the minimum repayment every month, or even the full balance to avoid paying interest.

If you have never had a credit card before it is unlikely that you will qualify for the best credit card deals, so you may wish to consider applying for bad credit cards that come with higher than average interest rates, such as the Vanquis card.

Don't let these high rates put you off, as if you ensure your balance is paid of fully each month, you will never have the interest applied. Also, if you make too many applications for credit within a small space of time your score can be damaged, so keep it simple.

Begin using your new credit card to pay for some of the things you would normally pay for by cash or debit card, while making sure you keep the money aside to cover the monthly bill. This will help to show lenders that you can effectively manage your credit while keeping on-top of your payments. Provided you pay off your credit card balance every month without fail, you will never pay a penny for using the card, and you will be building up a valuable credit history.

If you find you are unable to pay off your balance in full on some occasions, just make sure you pay off at least the minimum repayment amount. Even if you're struggling, this should be your priority as missing payments could lead to a default or County Court Judgement (CCJ) that haunt you for years. The same rule applies to your mortgage payments.

If you do find you are have difficulties with your repayment plan, the best thing you can do is speak to your lender, as they may be able to help you to change your repayment schedule.

The easiest and most effective way of making sure your credit cards are paid on time is to set up a monthly Direct Debit, allowing your payments to happen automatically.

# Sign Up To The Electoral Roll.

If you're not currently on the electoral roll, it is unlikely that you will be successful in your credit applications, so this is a must. Don't wait for your annual reminder, sign up online on the 'About my vote' website.

If you aren't eligible to vote (foreign nationals, etc), you can send each of the credit reference agencies proof of your residency and request that a note is added to verify this to increase your chances of obtaining credit.

# Monitor Your Credit Score

If you have been refused credit in the past, or you're simply curious about your credit status, you can request a report from any of the credit agencies. This does come with a fee, but this is generally less than ten pounds and can provide you with useful data. You can also contest any entries that you feel are not correct, so it's well worth spending some time going through the information as your score could have been tainted unnecessarily.

It's good practice to check your credit reports periodically. If possible, get a report from all three agencies, as there's no harm in doing so and this allows you to keep a close eye on every entry - such as credit card bills - in your report so you can spot any error that might be causing you problems. Repeat the check-up every 12 to 18 months, and try to avoid getting your report after making any important applications, as these can effect your score.

If you would rather avoid having to pay for a credit report, you

can get access to a simplified version for free by registering for a free monthly trial. This will require you to set up a Direct Debit or regular credit card payment using your payment details, but you won't have to pay anything as long as you close your account before the free period expires.

If you do find something in the report that you disagree with, you can request a change by writing to the agency. Although these amendments can be refused, you are entitled to add your own comments as a 'notice of correction', which may help you with future credit applications.

If something doesn't look right, write a concise, explanatory and factual letter to detail the error, and avoid writing something too wordy.

## Space Out Credit Applications.

One thing that you must remember is that each time you make an application to any form of credit, a credit search will be carried out, and making too many applications in a short space of time can have a bad effect on your score. You should therefore space out your credit applications, and even for things like car insurance, mobile phone contracts. This reinforces the bad credit cards choice, as you are more likely to be approved for products that are aimed at those with bad credit.

Moving house is also likely to disrupt your score, so if you're planning to make any important applications ensure they have completed by the time you come to relocate. You will also have a better score when you're earning a salary, so if you

planning to take time off due to maternity leave or suspected redundancy, make your applications beforehand.

## Joint Finances Can Affect Your Score

If your husband/wife has a bad credit score it shouldn't impact your finances, providing their data doesn't appear on your file.

By becoming 'financially linked' to someone through any product who has a bad score, such as a mortgage or a joint bank account, can cause negative effects to your score. Even simply opening a joint bills account when sharing a flat can mean you're co-scored.

The general rule of thumb is if one partner has a bad credit history, keep your finances separate wherever possible.

# CHAPTER 16

## GOOD OR BAD IS YOUR CREDIT SCORE?

In a nutshell, your credit score could range from anywhere between the low 300s to mid 800s. These are the general score ranges that are considered by credit bureaus and credit companies. It should be apparent from this that the 800 mark is the highest and the 300 is the lowest.

As you already know, having a poor credit score will determine how much it costs you to access credit. The lower that it gets the worse your interest rates and the more money that you spend, however, we looked at how companies will flock to target you and try and get as much money out of you as possible. These figures are set based on calculations that are done by the credit bureaus. Depending on your credit history, they will add up your debts and come up with a number that will help determine where you stand.

To help you understand the scores better, here is a breakdown of the credit score ranges and what each means. You might probably find that your credit score is pretty bad than you thought!

## 720 And Above-Excellent

When you have this score, you get the best interest rates and repayment terms for all loans. This score can come in handy if you are hoping to make some major purchases. You will avail credit without any problems and at the lowest possible rates. But then, this score is extremely hard to establish. You will have to put in a lot of effort to maintain this core and still, you will not come anywhere close to 800. The most you can wish is to come close to 720 and remain there for as long as possible.

## 680-719-Good

When you are in this category, you will get good rates and terms but not as good as those with excellent scores. With this score, you can get favorable mortgage terms. You might not face as much problem but will have to be ready to run around from company to company to have your credit approved. Again, this score is not very common. You need to put in extra effort to get it over the 680 mark. If because of some erroneous charges you are not able to cross this limit then you must try your best to get it cleared as soon as possible.

## 620-679-Average

When you are in this category, you can get fair mortgage terms and have it easy when buying smaller ticket items, (of course with no better rate than good and excellent scores). Take care not to slip down to the level where mortgage is unaffordable. You must keep an eye on your credit report and if there are unnecessary entries then immediately take action to fall back in your previous range. There can be many in this range or just miss out on it owing to bad entries. This range is average and most people with an average income will remain here.

## 580-619-Poor

When you are at this level, you only get credit on lenders' terms. You will probably pay more to access credit so be ready to pay more. Also, you should remember that you cannot access auto financing if your score goes lower than this range so you should work towards building it. This is where a large majority lie. Their score will be bad mostly owing to wrong entries. If you lie here then you will have a tough time getting credit in your budget limits and will have to be ready to pay up a lot of money.

## 500-579-Bad

If your credit score is in this range, access to credit will be quite high. Actually, if you are looking for a 30-year mortgage, you could be looking at, at least 3% higher interest rates than how much you would pay if you had good credit. On the other

hand, if you are looking for something short time like a 36-month auto loan, you might probably pay almost double the interest rate you would pay if you had good credit. So being here is probably the worst thing that can happen to your credit report. You cannot possibly be here and hope to get away with low-interest rates. That is next to impossible.

## Less than 500

If your credit score goes to this level, it is so bad that it might be almost impossible to get any type of financing. If you do, the interest rate will simply be unfathomable. You might have to spend 30 to 40 years trying to repay it. Your entire life will be dedicated to repaying a loan and might only get free by the time you are 50.

I am sure several of you are in this last range. But don't panic as help is at hand. You might wonder if it is possible for you to fix your score if you are in this category and the answer is, yes! It is possible for you to improve your credit score and possibly enter the good range.

Understand that no one wants to have his or her credit score bad for the simple reason that access to credit will be too costly. It will be the worst type of score for any person to have regardless of their borrowing habits. That's why it is paramount to take action when you start seeing inaccurate and unjustifiable entries in your report. If you spot errors that are causing you to be in this range then you must spring into action at the earliest. To help you understand what's at stake here, let me explain to you what is at stake and why you should start following up on everything reported on your

credit report otherwise you might end up paying more for credit than what you ought to; you don't have to learn the hard way.

To start with, I will explain some few facts about the credit reports just to put you on high alert on matters related to your credit.

A large proportion of credit reports have erroneous, unverifiable and incorrect entries; to be precise, 93% of credit reports have been found to have incorrect entries that affected credit score negatively. So, do you know what that means? It means that you and I could be having entries in our credit reports that we know nothing about; actually, we might simply discover that our credit score is ruined when our loan application is turned down. You need to look for these entries after gaining a free copy of your credit report. Now, as you have seen above on what each range of credit score means, by the time you get to the point of being turned down for a loan, your credit score is pretty much bad! You might start falling in the below 500 range and it will simply mean doom. The tiny details you see on your credit score that you don't understand where they came from could be the ones ruining your credit score. What happens is that lenders will often make some minor changes when reporting data to the credit bureaus some of which taint the credit consumer's financial reputation.

For instance, a change in the date of last activity on your credit report should be something you should start worrying about; when you have something derogatory appearing in the recent activity items, your credit score will be tainted. This might be

completely imaginary or a simple manipulation of your actual entry. You could even have noticed different creditors reporting the same debt multiple times in which case; your credit report will show that you are really sinking in debt even if this is not actually true. These might be some extra-large values, which will only make your score appear bad. You might also have noted the same creditor reporting the same debt in your credit report under various account numbers; this has the same effect as having multiple creditors reporting on the same debt.

Obviously, creditors could defend themselves as not knowing that these mistakes existed. However, they really care less about that because the worse of your credit score is, the more they charge you for credit. As was said before, they will stoop to any low just to get you in a fix. They will not care about your side of the story and stick to what they think is their right. So you need to be alert all throughout and do what is right for you.

The law requires that creditors can only keep information about your credit history for just 7 years. However, it isn't uncommon for lenders to keep this information for more than 10 years, which means such items will probably continue showing on your credit report year in year out, which in turn messes your credit score after which the lenders raise the interest rates you pay. They will not be accountable to anyone and will claim to have erased any information in regard to your credit scores. But they will keep using the data to bombard you with target specific emails and offers.

The answer to these inaccuracies in credit reports lies not in

sitting around and expecting your creditors to have mercy on you because they won't. This is the problem that most people suffer from. They will think the creditor will empathize with them and help them reduce their bad credit. But they will, in fact, be interested in ruining your credit score further so that they have a chance to pull more money from you. So, the best idea is to instead, start with you doing something about bettering your score and not wasting any more time.

In any case, why do these corporations (lenders) want you to pay them for something you shouldn't pay? You must understand how these companies will try and trick you and remain alert. If at any time you find out you are being cheated owing to mistakes and errors in your credit report, you need to spring into action and deal with them at the earliest. But what must you do to repair your credit as soon as possible?

The credit repair process can be complicated and frustrating especially if you don't know what to do. You might get lost easily and not have a clear direction. Actually, trying to dispute on your own without first understanding how to go about it could probably ruin your chances of ever succeeding; that's why most people probably give up on their trial because they never did their research well. You might ruin something that can be fixed easily and worsen your credit score in the process. So it is better to exercise precaution and try and do all the right things.

Knowing you have the right to dispute and actually disputing successfully are two totally different things; I will teach you what to do throughout the process if you are to emerge successful in the dispute process. The key to getting

derogatory items in your credit report deleted permanently is understanding and following the tested and tried credit repair process otherwise you might simply start going in circles where you get an item removed and later restored in the credit report within 60 days.

# CHAPTER 17

# 14 MOST DESTRUCTIVE ITEMS ON YOUR CREDIT REPORT

**W**e will explore ways to mitigate the most destructive negative items that will affect your credit report. Some of these topics are very complex and it is beyond the scope of this book to offer legal and financial advice as to how to deal with them. However, we do look at various possible ways to fight them.

In spite of all the information on the Internet and suggestions from other dubious sources, there is no silver bullet solution that will easily and automatically remove any of these negative items from your credit report. There is no magic secret that only a few brilliant people in the world know about. There is no credit repair agency that can honestly guarantee it either. The reason is that if negative information is accurate, you cannot force the reporting agency, nor the IRS, nor the credit bureau to remove it. You can request it, and you can try some loopholes that may work, but you cannot force it.

All the solutions provided here have worked for other people; however, they may not always work, for all people, in all situations. You will need to be the judge as to what might be best for you.

The good news is that everyday people get these destructive items removed from their credit report. You can do so too with a little effort, and in some cases, a little luck.

1. Late Payments – a late payment results in a delinquency mark on your credit standing. This is the most common negative item on credit reports. Items such as being 30 days late on your mortgage payment are significant, and can result in a substantial drop in your credit score. Payment history accounts for about 35% of your credit score so that late payments will have a major negative impact.

   If you are currently behind on payments, ask the creditor if you can negotiate for a lower settlement amount, which includes their removing the late payments from your credit record after you have settled your debt. If they still want the full amount then you may need to catch up before you can do anything else

   If you cannot pay back your late payments, ask the creditor if you can work out a new payment plan that includes removal of the late payment information after you finish making a set number of payments, such as the first twelve monthly payments for the next year.

   If they still want the full amount first, then you will have

to get up to date on the amount owed. Once you are up to date with your payments, you can contact the creditor and plead your case to remove the negative late payment information. If you have a long term relationship with them, let them know. If you have a short term relationship with them, focus on your good record up until the current situation. Your goal is to convince them that you are a good customer and want to remain a good customer. Be polite and calm, and ask that they remove the negative information they placed on your credit record. If they agree, get the agreement in writing. Their contact information is located on your credit report under "Creditor Contacts."

Once a late payment gets on your credit report, it may remain there for up to 7 years. However, if paid in full, it may just say "paid" on your credit report.

2. Collections – An account is usually sent to collections six months after the first missed payment, and will remain on your credit report for up to 7 years. If you pay off the full amount owed, the account status will change on your credit report to "paid collection." If you settle for less, the account status may say "settled for less than full balance."

3. Charge-offs – most charge offs are the result of not paying a credit card bill for several months. Typically after 180 days of non-payments, the creditor (after hitting your credit report with several late or no payment notations) will write off the debt as a loss on their books, and cancel your account.

4.  Short-sales

    A short-sale is a situation where you negotiate with the bank regarding the sale of your house. If the bank is receptive to a short-sale (and they usually are since it is better than a foreclosure), it will work with you and the buyer to determine a mutually acceptable price for the home.

5.  Loan modifications – a loan modification is when the lender agrees to modify some or all of the original terms of the loan. The changes may include extending the length of the loan, changing the interest rate, or changing the monthly payment. It allows a home owner to keep their home when they can't make their mortgage payments at the current rate. How the loan modification affects your credit score is dependent on the details of the modification.

6.  Judgments - Judgments can be tricky since they cover so much ground and you are usually dealing with the court system. The first thing to know is that the courts typically don't provide judgment information to the credit bureaus. They get it either through third parties, or through their own search of public records. They then record it as they see fit. So it is possible that a judgment may be listed differently (or not at all) by each credit bureau. That means you may have to handle each credit bureau differently as well.

7.  Wage garnishment – if you owe money and the creditor sues you and wins a judgment against you, the creditor can have your wages garnished directly from your

employer. Federal law limits the garnishment amount to 25% of take-home pay after taxes. A wage garnishment judgment can remain on your credit report for seven years.

8. Car repossession – A repossession occurs when loan payments are missed and the creditor takes back possession of the car. The creditor will then sell the car and if the sale price does not cover the remainder of the loan, then the creditor may choose to forgive the debt, or continue to seek the rest of the amount from you. That leftover amount may also include such costs as fees for the repossession, storage, towing, charges for cleaning the car and preparing it to sell, registration fees, cost to sell or auction the car and more. In some cases, it may end up costing you more to let the car be repossessed than to continue to make the payments.

9. Student Loans – A student loan is used for the purpose of paying for tuition, housing and books while the student is still in school. It differs from a traditional loan in that the interest rate on a student loan is usually lower, and the student can often defer payments until he/she is no longer in school.

10. Medical Bills – The effect of medical bills on household finances often gets overlooked. However, it is a major problem in America today. According to nationally published reports, in 2013 alone, 56 million Americans reported having trouble paying their medical bills, 15 million used up their life savings paying medical bills, 1.7 million declared bankruptcy because of medical

bills, and nearly half of all late payments were due to medical bills. If you are one of these people you can see that you have a lot of company.

11. Tax Liens – A tax lien is a tool the government uses to let other creditors know that it has an interest in your property resulting from unpaid taxes. With the drop in the economy, tax liens have exploded in recent years. The Taxpayer Advocate found that the IRS had filed over 300,000 tax liens in 2013 alone.

12. Bankruptcies – a bankruptcy is by far the single most damaging action to your credit score. In fact, your score can drop as much as 300 points after a bankruptcy. Most Chapter 7 and 11 bankruptcies remain on your credit report for as many as ten years although Chapter 13's often come off after 7 years. After the Order of Discharge (the court order at the end of the bankruptcy proceeding) is filed, all the accounts that were discharged will be marked as "Included in Bankruptcy" on your report, and will remain on it for up to 7 years.

13. Foreclosure – Dealing with the legal and financial aspects of a foreclosure is beyond the scope of this book, so we recommend that you seek expert advice on any major financial decisions. There may even be low cost housing counselors in your area who can advise you as well.

14. Closed Accounts – Many people assume that when an account is closed or inactive, that it no longer affects your credit status. However, if an account is closed while delinquent, the negative information will remain

on your credit report for up to 7 years. Even if the account was in good standing when it closed, it could still negatively impact your score. Lenders want to see a long credit history and a low percentage of available credit being used. Closing an account may shorten your credit history and increase the percentage of available credit. If you are worried about having too many open accounts, be selective about which ones to close. Make certain there is no outstanding balance at closing, and request confirmation that the account has been closed.

If the closed account still shows a balance, you can contact the original creditor and negotiate a settlement. Tell them that you are willing to pay a percentage of the debt if they are willing to remove the negative information from your credit report. The larger the debt is, the more likely they will be to negotiate, and even settle for a percentage of the amount owed. The more aged the debt is, the more leverage you have in the negotiation. If the debt is over three years old you can try offering 25% of the debt owed; at two to three years old, try 50%, and for less than two years, 75%. Your results will be better if you can make the payment in a lump sum. If you need to make payments, you may have to pay a higher percentage or even the entire amount. Regardless of the settlement amount, always make sure that you get in writing that they will remove the damaging information from your credit report as a condition of the settlement.

# CHAPTER 18

## WHAT LAWS EXIST TO REPAIR THE CREDIT?

The Fair Credit Reporting Act gives you the right to:

- Know the name, address, and phone number of anyone who has seen your credit record over the past two years for employment purposes and the right to know who has reviewed your credit information for any other purpose over the past 12 months

- Have a credit bureau notify employers who reviewed your credit record over the past two years, or anyone else who may have reviewed your file over the previous six months, of any corrections or deletions made to your credit file, if you so request and provide the credit-reporting agency the names of all companies and individuals you want notified

- Have a brief explanatory statement added to credit file with regard to information in your file that you dispute but have been unsuccessful in changing or deleting

- To have a bankruptcy deleted after ten years

- Be notified by a company that it has requested an investigative report on you

## The CARD Act of 2009

The role the CARD Act of 2009 plays in credit repair is indirect in nature. Rather than giving you a mechanism for challenging the credit-reporting agencies, it acts as "preventative medicine" by guaranteeing you equitable treatment and some ability to control their own destiny. In short, the act will make it less likely for you to get into credit card debt because of abusive practices by credit card issuers. Below, I list the key provisions of the act.

### Stops Surprise Rate Increases and Changes in Terms

- No more indiscriminate interest rate hikes or universal default on your credit card simply because you were late on another debt

- If your rate is increased for cause (such as a 60-day delinquency), the credit card company must review your payment record periodically and adjust the rate to its previous level if you have made your payments on time for six months

- Credit card issuers cannot increase your rates in the first year

- Promotional rates are permitted, but must remain in force for a minimum of six months

- Rates and terms may be changed, but a 45-day notice is required

## Prohibits Unnecessary Fees

- Card issuers are no longer permitted to charge you a fee to pay a credit card debt, by mail, telephone, or electronic transfer, the exception being live services to make rush payments

- Over limit fees are banned unless you choose to allow the issuer to complete over-limit transactions, and even if you do, the act limits these fees to one per billing cycle

- Fcharges must be reasonable and proportional to the transgression

- Improved protections against exorbitant fees on low limit, high-fee credit cards

## Requires Consumer-Oriented Application and Timing of Card Payments

- If you pay more than your minimum payment, the excess must be applied first to the credit card balance with the highest rate of interest (typically the cash advance balance)

- Card issuers cannot set early morning deadlines for payments

- Statements must be mailed twenty-one days before the due

## No More "Double-Cycle" Billing

- Stops the dubious practice of basing finance charges on the average balance over two billing cycles, which penalizes you if you pay your balance in full

- Prohibits late fees caused by delays in crediting your payment

- Payments made at local branches must be credited same-day

- Mandates that credit card companies evaluate your ability to pay before issuing your credit card or raising your credit limit

## Requires Improved Disclosure of Credit Terms and Conditions

- Mandates that you be given 45 days' notice of interest rate, fee, and finance charge increases

- Disclosures must be provided upon your card's renewal if terms have changed

- Credit card companies must disclose the length of time to retire your debt and total interest expense that results from making only the minimum payment

- Each billing statement must disclose payment due dates and applicable late payment fees

## Makes Industry Practices More Transparent

- Card issuers must make their credit card agreements available on the Internet, and furnish those agreements to the Federal Reserve Board, which will also publish

them on their website

- The Federal Reserve Board is required to review the consumer credit card market, the terms of credit card agreements, the practices of credit card issuers, and the cost and availability of credit to consumers

- Mandates the Federal Trade Commission to prevent the deceptive marketing of so-called free credit reports

## Precludes the Exploitation of Young People

- Persons under the age of twenty-one must prove their ability to pay or provide a co-signer aged 21 or older to or their credit card application will not be approved

- Limits prescreened offers of credit to persons under 21 years of age

- Credit limit increases on co-signed accounts must also be approved by the person jointly responsible for the debt

## Provides for Higher Penalties

- Implements more severe penalties for any company violating the Truth in Lending Act for credit card customers

## Gift Card Rules

- Mandates that gift cards be valid for five years and eliminates the practice of graduated reductions in card value and hidden fees

## Protects Entrepreneurs

- The Federal Reserve is required to study the use of credit cards by small businesses and make recommendations for regulatory and legislative changes

- The act establishes Small Business Information Security Task Force to address the information technology security needs of small business and develop measures to prevent the loss of credit card data

## Mandates Financial Literacy

- Mandates the development of a comprehensive plan to improve financial literacy education and the summarization of existing financial literacy initiatives

It is always a good idea to attach a copy of your credit report with any correspondence you send to a credit-reporting agency with the error(s) highlighted or circled.

Avoid including anything in your correspondence that is unprofessional or frivolous in nature. The credit reporting agencies can reject frivolous disputes. However, the credit-reporting agency must inform you in writing of their refusal to investigate and include an explanation of why it views your request as frivolous or irrelevant. Maintaining a business-like approach will add credibility to your allegations of inaccuracies.

# CHAPTER 19

## CREDIT REPAIR SCAMS AND HOW TO AVOID THEM

**M**ortgage loan qualification requirements are stricter today than in the past - FHA / VA and Conventional Home Loan sources are requiring ever higher FICO scores so the average applicant may need to improve their credit report before they can qualify for a home loan. With the demand for housing beginning to grow, it makes a very ripe market for scammers. Most popular credit repair scams promise to wipe your credit report clean of all negative information. They usually charge an up front fee, sometimes as much as $1,500 for their service. Often all the scammers will do is dispute all the negative information on your credit report. This is something you can do on your own for free.

Another "We will fix it" scam for a fee is to tell you that they will get you a new social security number. The idea is with a new number most credit agencies would have to start a new file under that number with your name and it wouldn't have the negative information that may have been reported under your old SS number. The truth is, the Social Security Administration almost never agrees to assign a new SS number to an individual who already has a file and number. What these "credit repair" scammers are doing is filing with the IRS for an EIN (Employer Identification Number) under your name. It's also a nine-digit number that looks like a social security number, but is actually a number assigned to a business. This number is used by the IRS to identify companies for tax payment purposes.

If you fall for this one, the conse□uences are far reaching. By using an EIN as your SS number, you change how your income is reported to the IRS. You'll find it's a big problem when you retire and the Social Security Administration has no record of your work history. Not only will your social security checks be in jeopardy, you may find yourself accused of conspiring to commit fraud with possible jail time in your future. Remember, there is no magic formula to repairing your credit score, and no big secrets that only a credit repair company has access to. Credit score repair is actually a fairly simple process of writing letters and then following up, and it can be done by anyone. The scammers are out there, and they want your money so be informed and don't be a victim.

# The Solution To Post-Bankruptcy Bad Credit

Doing credit repair after you have had a bankruptcy is probably one of the smartest things you can do for your credit profile. If you believed the story your attorney told you after your bankruptcy that your credit report would take care of itself, you are probably regretting that. No doubt your credit report does not look like you hoped it would after your bankruptcy.

Self credit repair is your solution. Don't be misled by credit repair companies that claim they can get your bankruptcy removed from your report. The fact of the matter is that when you fill out a loan application you will most likely have to declare if you have had a bankruptcy within the last 7 years anyhow. If you don't disclose this, you are committing fraud. You should not commit fraud! It is dangerous.

So, your bankruptcy is discharged and your credit report still looks like a mess. You still have accounts that show up with balances on them when they were included in your bankruptcy and should show no balance. Other accounts show a balance of zero, but they still have a negative rating on them. You are probably in a situation where you pretty much need to dispute anything that is negative on your credit report. You have the right to dispute anything you don't feel is reporting 100% accurately because you have the right to have everything on your report be 100% accurate. That is the law found in the Fair Credit Reporting Act.

You should already have a copy of your credit report. You can get this online or you can probably get it from the lender that

denied your credit. Just ask them for it. They can usually scan it and email it to you as a PDF file. Once you have your report, read it and decide what you think you need to dispute. This can be a bit of a daunting task, especially if you don't really know how to read the report. If you got your report from you loan officer, call them and ask them to help you decipher the report. You might even be able to get them to put an 'X' next to anything on your report that they think is hurting your profile. Since you don't want to dispute anything that is helping your profile, this will give you a good place to start deciding what you are going to dispute in your Credit Repair letters. You can dispute collections, charge offs, public records, bad debts. As I stated, if you have had a bankruptcy, you probably have a lot of accounts on your report that still show balances when they should not since they were included in your bankruptcy. Start with these.

Now that you know what you want to dispute, you need to write credit dispute letters. This is basically what a credit repair company would do for you, but you can do it on your own pretty easily. There is software available on the web that you can purchase and there are free sites that you can use. You should seek these out if you would like to save yourself a lot of time. If you have a lot of time on your hands (who does?) you can write the credit repair letters out yourself.

Sending out basic credit dispute letters is typically very effective, especially if the letters really look like they are from you and not created by a program. Some software will actually help you do that. You don't want the text and font to be the same on all the letters. Change it up a bit.

From personal experience helping people send out basic credit dispute letters, I can attest that they can be very effective in getting your report to be more accurate, and in improving your credit score tremendously.

## What Everyone With Bad Credit Should Know About Credit Repair Services

If you're one of the millions of people in America with bad or damaged credit, don't despair. There are several things you can do to improve your credit. If you're looking for information about how to repair your credit and credit repair services, you've come to the right place. In this article we'll discuss the definition of bad credit and the benefits of using credit repair services. By the end of this article you should be able to start repairing your credit today, whether you choose to do so on your own, or hire a professional service to assist you.

## What Is Considered Bad Credit?

Most lenders define bad credit as any credit score lower than 620. After the subprime mortgage fiasco, some lenders are even raising that bar to 640. In addition to your payment patterns and amount of outstanding debt, your time on the job and your time living at your current address make up a portion of your creditworthiness. People who stay at the same employer and residence longer are considered more creditworthy than those who change jobs or move frequently.

If you are interested in improving your credit, it's in your best interest to know what your credit score is, even if you are afraid to find out! Order a copy of your credit report and make sure you get reports from all three major credit reporting agencies: EÐuifax, Experian and Transunion. Some lenders use the top score and some use a blended score so it is important to know what is on each report. Once you know where you stand you can begin the process of repairing your credit.

## Benefits Of Credit Repair Services

Credit repair services can help in a number of ways. Many of them offer packages that include obtaining your credit report, looking for inaccuracies and contacting the reporting agencies on your behalf. The primary benefit of credit repair services is that they save you time and effort. Most of what a credit repair service can do, you can do for yourself. But just like many services, the benefit is in convenience and saving time. It's akin to repairing your own car; it is technically possible for you to do it yourself, but if you lack knowledge and experience in repairing cars, you could probably save a lot of time and frustration by paying someone else to do it for you.

There are credit repair service companies that do not offer a true value because they use ineffective and/or outdated tactics. Some of the large and well-known companies are guilty of this. Make sure you investigate the credit repair service that you're considering and find out exactly what they offer. Get all of their claims in writing and find out what their

refund policy is. Do not pay any fees up front (with the exception of a one-time set-up fee), and when in doubt, walk away.

Credit problems can be difficult to deal with, but help is available. The first step is determining your credit score and looking at the contents of your credit reports. Then decide if you want to take on the task of disputing negative listings yourself, or if you want to bring in a professional credit repair service to help. Credit repair services can save you time and effort although they can't really do anything for you that you couldn't do for yourself. When shopping for a credit repair service, make sure you investigate them thoroughly to protect yourself from any scams. With the information in this article you should be better informed about the best way to repair your credit.

# CHAPTER 20

# REASONS FOR EXCELLENT CREDIT

The reason why many fail to achieve their financial goals is their inability to manage their credit. In America, a good credit score can be a financial tool you can use to leverage the playing field in our capitalistic society. Research reveals that an average credit score in the US is at an all-time high of 695; though this varies in terms of the model, age, population, states, income levels, and other factors. Meanwhile, a score of 720 and above is tagged excellent and less than 660 is regarded as a poor credit score.

Some people wonder if they really need to keep good credit. Many financial experts will tell you that credit doesn't matter if you plan to be out of debt, because you won't be borrowing money going forward, so what does your credit matter?

There are three elements of money that eat away the principle; they are taxes, interest, and insurance. These three elements make up the majority of where our money goes throughout our lifetime. It's true that most people in the workingclass will make over a million dollars in their lifetime, but the question remains: How can you retain most of what you've earned? My suggestion is, get a good CPA or tax advisor, make it a habit of shopping for insurance and invest in getting those credit scores above 750.

Ideally speaking, it would be great to get the best interest rates for those major purchases, and having excellent credit will definitely cut the expenses over a long period of time. Here are a few things to consider as you make those major purchases. When you think of excellent FICO scores, think of how much money you will save.

## Buying A House

Someday, especially if you are young, you will want to buy a place of your own, and that will require some high standards when it comes to credit and your credit score. Most lenders require a minimum credit score of 680 to qualify for a fixed rate mortgage.

You always want to shoot for a fixed rate as it limits your monthly payment to a fixed amount, so there are no surprises down the road. If you choose a 30-year fixed rate, keep your options open to paying it like a 15-year mortgage due to the fact that the interest on a 30-year mortgage will have a compound effect.

Take the time to go over your amortization schedule so you can clearly see how your interest payments are calculated against the principal payments.

## Financing A Car

Similar to buying a house, you will need a good credit score to finance the purchase of your next vehicle. Most banks and even car dealers will offer you a better rate if your credit score is higher. And obviously, we all want the lowest rate when borrowing money.

My suggestion for financing any type of highly depreciating asset like a car is to borrow only up to 60-70 percent on the car's loan value. This provides you with an equity safety net which will help you get a jump start on paying the loan off before the value of the car can drop too much.

Note: If you plan on purchasing a home DO NOT finance a vehicle until you have gone over the numbers on what your debt to income ratio would be if you purchased a home.

## Getting A Job

Like it or not, many employers have began running credit checks on their candidates. In fact, 47 percent of employers admitted to running your credit when you apply for a job. After all, if you're being hired to work for someone, they want to know how responsible you are with your own money. This is a good indicator that your employer cares about habits including: can you manage your responsibilities, are you timely and are you an integrity-laden person?

At this time there is no data suggesting that employers are using FICO scores as a factor in their decision-making process.

## Starting a Business

Every year, thousands of Americans decide to start their own business. However, getting a business up and running isn't always easy and usually takes some significant funding to get going and stay afloat.

Depending on the type of business you want to start, you may need to have your local community bank to help you make your dreams a reality and succeed. Even if you plan to borrow money in your business' name, most banks require a credit check and evaluation of the partners of the business; because after all, you are the one who will be making the decisions.

## Emergencies

Dave Ramsey always says that many times in life, "Murphy shows up at your door and wants to stay awhile." He is referring to the concept of Murphy's Law. The infamous statement that, "If something can go wrong, it will go wrong."

We all find ourselves in this situation at some point in ourlives when things just seem to happen for the worst. Your car breaks down two weeks from payday, your furnace goes out in the middle of winter or worse, you lose your job. Now what? Our philosophy for all our readers is that we encourage living debt free as much as possible, but sometimes you just have to borrow some money to make things work.

# Insurance

Car insurance companies are another group that have adopted the use of credit scores to help determine risk. Studies have shown that drivers with low credit scores are more likely to file insurance claims. And since claims cost the insurance companies money, they want to make sure that the people more apt to file them are charged accordingly. For this reason, the vast majority of auto insurance companies factor in your score when drawing up a policy. The lower your score is, the more you will have to pay in insurance premiums.

Credit card companies also take your credit score into account,which is something most people were aware of, but not everyone realizes the extent of. Since a credit card is similarto a loan, in that you are granted a line of credit that youare required to pay back with interest, it makes sense thatcredit card companies factor your score into how much credit you can get approved for and at what interest rate. What many fail to realize is that these figures are not fixed. A credit card company likes to include a "universal default" provision in their contracts in which they reserve the right to monitoryour credit reports and increase the credit card interest rate if you have late payments or other negative items added to your credit reports, even if they are completely unrelated to the credit card account.

Since credit card debt is unsecured and can be dismissed in a bankruptcy, credit card companies work hard to make sure that if your finances get out of control, they are going to collect as much money from you as possible. Any indication

that you might be having trouble making payments and they may start working to offset any future losses.

As you can see, a good credit score opens up a world of opportunities and has benefits many people didn't even realize were there. On the flip side, a bad credit score can be a hugeroadblock causing people to have to work much harder injust about every facet of their finances.

# CHAPTER 21

# HOW TO REBUILD A GOOD CREDIT HISTORY

Having a good credit history is a good thing that everybody will yearn to have, and given the benefits that come with a good history, it is no doubt why many people are rushing to clean up their reports. It is without doubt that one will have easy access to loans and other forms of credit provided the history on one's file shows a good report. But there are some things that are needed to get it right.

First, you need to ensure that you have no negative information on your file. Negative information such as collections, late pays, charge-offs, inquiries, court judgments and other negative entries sends your score down and affects your rating negatively - this is part of what makes up your history. Thus it becomes imperative that you try to get rid of information that will help in boosting your present score and put your history in a good perspective.

But that's not all. You need to take measures to control the everyday active part of your personal finances too. For instance, you may discover that having 4 or 5 credit cards has actually been hurtful to your file rather than beneficial.

## Rebuild & Keep Good Credit Ratings By Understanding Your Credit Cards

Secured Credit Card is similar to a prepaid credit card since the funds you are using are actually yours and not the issuer of the credit card. Generally people who apply for secured credit card or prepaid credit card are people with poor credit or unemployed. Prepaid Credit Card spending limit is the amount of money you loaded to the card. There are no interest or finance charges on a prepaid card. With secured credit card, your credit line could be from 50% to 100% of your deposit depending on the institution giving you the secured credit. Therefore the company giving you the secured credit card has zero risk.

Secured credit card can be very beneficial because it gives you an opportunity to rebuild your credit history and you are able to make purchases just as if you had an unsecured credit card. Many companies re uire that you have a credit card to make purchases, such as car rental, airline tickets, etc. Ensure that the company issuing the secured credit, routinely reports customers' payment history to any of the three main credit bureaus namely Experian, E uifax and Trans Union. This reporting to the credit bureaus will rebuild your credit history over time.

Closing unnecessary accounts and consolidating your bills to make payments more manageable could be an advantage financially. By not applying for too much credit within a short period of time is another factor that will help in rebuilding your credit rating. Additionally, even though secured credit is like prepaid cards, they do have certain fees attached.

Benefits are similar to that of an unsecured credit card, such as usually being paid interest on your balance in the bank, using Automated Teller Machines (ATM) to make deposits, withdrawals, and making purchases at participating merchants. Following the above steps will strengthen your credit rating.

Unsecured Credit Cards are issued to individuals with good to excellent credit rating. Credit ratings depend on certain criteria, such as one's ability to repay loans. These criteria include payment history, employment history, and financial stability. Individuals with excellent credit will most likely receive a lower interest rate. A major factor in maintaining excellent credit is making your loan payments on time thus avoiding late fee penalties.

Customers should read the credit agreement to ensure that they understand their obligation to the creditor. Making payments on time will strengthen your credit rating. Unsecured credit cards has numerous advantages such as low interest rates, high credit limit, business name options, no annual fees, and low APRs on balance transfers up to 12 months. Closing unnecessary accounts and consolidating your bills to make payments more manageable could be an

advantage financially. By not applying for too much credit within a short period of time is another factor that will help in maintaining a good credit rating.

Rebuilding your credit takes time, patience, and consistency. If you consistently pay your bills on time, you will see an improvement in your credit ratings over time.

Applying for secured credit card can be very beneficial because it gives you an opportunity to rebuild your credit history, and you are able to make purchases just as if you had an unsecured credit card. Many companies require that you have a credit card to make purchases, such as car rental, airline tickets, etc.

## Business Credit Card

Business credit cards are very popular for small business owners because of the many benefits they offer. Benefits includes 0% Intro APR on balance transfers, no annual fees, high credit limit, low interest rates, cash rewards, bonus miles, free online account management to choosing card design etc., At iCreditOnlin dotcom we have some of the best business credit cards from American Express, Advantage, Chase, Bank One, Bank of America, Discover, Citibank, Household Bank and more, with online credit card approval. Why waste time going to a bank when you can get a decision in less than 60 seconds with secure online credit card application. Online Credit Card Approval with Online Credit Card Application is fast and easy!

## Student Credit Card

Having a student credit card while still living at home or attending school away from home can be an advantage. It gives the student the opportunity to establish credit at an early age and to start asserting their independence. It comes in handy in case of emergency, it is less trouble and safer to carry a student credit card than to carry cash. Parents find student credit cards to be very convenient. They are able to make deposits to their children's account while they are away from home. Students should be careful with their credit card receipts to avoid identity thief.

If you consistently pay your bills on time, obtaining students credit cards is a good way to established credit rating and start building a good credit history while in school. Establishing and maintaining a good credit rating will make it easy to purchase a car, a home or obtaining a personal loan in the future. For students who are not committed to their financial obligation, getting a student credit card is not a good idea. Running up balances, finding yourself in debt, unable to make monthly payments will destroy your credit rating.

Student's credit cards generally have high interest rates. At iCreditOnline.com we offer some of the best student credit cards from Chase and Discover with 0% APR introductory rate for 6 months, no annual fees and online account access. Online credit card approval with online credit card application is fast and easy!

## Explanation Of Some Of The Credit Cards We Offer:

0% Intro APR Credit Card or Balance Transfer Credit Card gives you the benefit of using this credit card without making any interest payment on the principal for a stated period of time. This credit card is marketed to individuals with good credit rating who want to transfer balance from a high interest credit card to a 0% intro APR credit card.

Cash Rewards or Cash Back Credit Card earns a percentage on purchases made. This reward or cash back is credited to your account.

Debit Card takes the place of carrying a checkbook or cash. This card is used like a credit card with certain limitations, such as not being able to rent a car. Purchase transactions are contingent upon having enough funds in your checking or savings account to cover the purchase. Verification of funds requires entering your Personal Identification Number (PIN) at a point-of-sale terminal.

Low interest credit card saves you money. Having a good credit rating Dualifies you for some of the best low APR credit card offers.

Prepaid Credit Card spending limit is the amount of money you loaded to the card. There are no interest or finance charges on a prepaid card. Therefore the company giving you the prepaid credit card has zero risk. Generally people who apply for prepaid credit card are people with poor credit or unemployed.

Secured Credit Card is secured by the amount of funds you have in your account. Your credit line could be from 50% to 100% of your deposit depending on the institution giving you the secured credit.

Unsecured Credit Card is issued to individuals with good to excellent credit rating. Credit ratings depend on certain criteria, such as one's ability to repay loans. These criteria include payment history, employment history, and financial stability. Individuals with excellent credit will most likely receive a lower interest rate and can receive instant online credit card approval. A major factor in maintaining excellent credit is making your loan payments on time thus avoiding late fee penalties.

Travel Rewards Credit Card benefits may include travel accident insurance, free rental car collision/loss damage insurance, rebate on gasoline purchases, freQuent flyer points or bonus miles towards airline flights, free Quarterly and annual account summaries.

## How To Qualify For And Establish Good Credit

The credit score shows someone how desirable they are to a lender. When a lender sizes you up to determine how much credit, if any to grant you, it usually looking at your credit report and measures your past credit history performance based on your credit score. Generally, a lender usually looks at these 3 keys areas: character, capacity and capital

(sometime known as 3Cs) to project how responsibly you handle your credit obligations. Hence, to Dualify for and establish good credit, you need to get good score in these 3 areas. Let discuss it one by one.

## Character

When you promptly pay principal and interest on your mortgage, student loans, credit card and other loans, you established a good character. By demonstrating a strong sense of character, you persuade the lender to trust that you will make a good-faith effort to pay your bills even if you run into financial difficulties.

## Capacity

Capacity measures your financial ability to assume a certain amount of debt. Whenever you apply for a loan, the lender will ask for your annual income statement and your investment portfolio and he/she also want to get to know your other income sources. Many banks set minimum income reDuirements that your must meet to qualify for certain dollars of credit. The higher your total earning, the larger your credit capacity will be. Besides considering your sources of income, lender also takes into consideration of your existing debts. They prefer it if no more than a maximum of 36 percent of your income pays your total fixed expenses, and if no more that 28 percent of your income pays for housing, either mortgage or rent. The more debt you incur, the less credit lenders extend.

## Capital

Lenders consider stocks, bonds, mutual funds, real estate, collectibles, cars and other asset as your capital that they can disposal to retire your debts if your character and capacity do not prove sufficient. Sometimes, lender may need you to pledge your capital/asset for your loan if your character and capacity are not sufficient to persuade lender to approve your application.

# CHAPTER 22

# CONSEQUENCES OF NOT PAYING YOUR DEBT

**W**hat happens when you go into serious delinquency or default on your loans? Well, it depends on the type of loan. With cars and houses, they can be repossessed by the bank. With consumer debt, you are often going to have to declare bankruptcy to wipe out old debts if you are far enough underwater.

Government-backed student loans, however, are a whole different beast. They can NOT be removed via bankruptcy. After 270 days of no payments, they are officially in default and sit there like a bad acne breakout on your credit report, making your score look yucky. Some student loan companies will then turn the loans over to official debt collection companies, which start yammering your phone away about late payments. In addition, you'll be on the hook for their own special fees. Yay.

You might have to try the 'secured credit card' trick to build up your credit again after this kind of financial disaster. Some people want to reach out to a debt settlement company or try to get a payday loan, but please don't! Debt settlement companies have to get paid too, you know, and they'll come after your money one way or another. Most of them are scams. The only honest ones are non-profits, and even those are doubtful. Payday loans charge sickening interest rates of more than 500% in some cases, so for a $1,000 payday loan, you'll be screwed out of more than $5,000. What kind of sense does that make? Stay far away from them.

If you don't pay your credit cards, they sit untouched with the original creditor for about six months. An original creditor is a bank like Chase, Citi, Capital One, Discover, or American Express. If you keep making payments, even if it's just $10 a month, the account will remain open with the original creditor.

But if you stop making payments for six months, then the original creditor turns the debt along with its collected interest over to a debt collection company. They then attempt to collect the debt for another six months. By now, you've not made a single payment for a year. If no payments are made, then your debt, with any added fees and other expenses from the debt collection company, is then turned over to a law office, where a judgment is brought against you in the form of a lawsuit. The law office represents either the original creditor or the debt buying company. The amount of small claims lawsuits based on collecting past debts has increased significantly in the past ten years, and now there are specialty

law firms devoted solely to debt collecting from average people. Well, at least we don't have debtors' prisons anymore.

If this happens, the creditor or debt collector is the plaintiff, and you become the defendant. You can even go to trial and meet with a lawyer to set up court-ordered payment plans based on your actual financial paperwork that you bring to the courthouse. Keep in mind that there is often interest included even after judgment is brought against you.

If you still fail to pay, a lien could be put on your property and your wages could be garnished from your current paycheck. It's legal in most states to garnish up to 25% of your wages. However, if you are seriously buried, you should know that the great state of Texas does not allow wage garnishment so if you are considering a move, Texas might be the place!

Being informed about this entire process will help you make better decisions on repairing your credit before bills go to collections. Dealing with debt collectors is its own game, so let's take a look. It's a bit different than just dealing with a credit card company. The rules have changed.

## Make Debt Collectors Go Away

Unfortunately, debt collector companies just won't take your word for it that you're going through a rough time or that they need to leave you alone. They do need to see proof. Collectors love paperwork! The more proof in writing, the better. So, before calling up your debt collector to give them the complete story of why you can't pay, get yourself prepared.

Spend the time gathering up all of your financial paperwork.

Get copies of your taxes that show your income and your financial situation. Gather your doctor's bills, your SSDI paperwork, your paystubs, and, if you're sharing an income or living on someone else's SSI, all the paperwork that goes along with that person.

Then, once you've gathered all your paperwork, call up your collector. Keep an eye on the prompts on the phone until you get to the customer service department. Be prepared to wait a long time on the phone. Just set aside the time to devote to this. Be polite, but brief and direct. Tell the representative that you can't pay and you have the proof you can't. Ask them how you can get them the paperwork so they can attach it to your file. Maybe you can send it in an e-mail as a PDF attachment or mail it or fax it to them? Get the name of the representative and the state (or country) where they are. Takedown your account number. Ask if you need to provide any other paperwork as proof of the inability to pay. If they tell you that you need something, comply with that. Ask if they can put a financial hardship status on your account. If so, that's great. Many collectors don't.

After you hang up, immediately follow the representative's instructions to send the paperwork to the collector. Keep all originals and only send copies. Put a note in your calendar to call in two weeks to follow up.

After two weeks, call up the customer service department again. Explain that you spoke to "Name" and have they received all of your paperwork? Make sure every last piece of paper is attached to your file.

The third step is to put your name on their "Do Not Call" list.

VERY IMPORTANT: Keep in mind that they won't call about important stuff, either, like courtesy calls notifying you that your balance has changed. So, do this with caution. Yes, the phone calls are uber annoying. But, that's the primary legal way of contacting you.

You actually need to send your request not to be contacted in writing. Write or type legibly on a blank sheet of paper:

To Capital One,

Please put my name on your "Do Not Call" list. Please remove my name from all call lists. I understand that I will not receive any phone calls.

Thank you,

Your Name

Keep a copy, in case you need it for legal purposes. After you've mailed your request to the collector, wait three weeks for them to receive it and attach the request to your file. Your account will be flagged "Do Not Call" if it's been done properly. Follow up and call the collector to make sure your account has been flagged. Ask the representative if you need to do anything else to make sure you are not contacted.

Throughout this whole negotiating process, continue to send what payments you can. Yes, you can absolutely send small payments to a debt collector, even if it's just $10 or $20 a month. It buys you a little time to change your financial situation. Don't give up and don't just stop sending payments.

You can also settle with debt collectors. Ask them about settlement options and start with less than 50% of the debt owed. They might come back with a counter-offer. After you agree to the settlement, stick with its terms to the letter or you will be on the hook for the whole amount and you can't renegotiate for a new settlement. If you do this, make sure you have them put Paid in Full on your credit report if possible.

If your financial situation changes at any point (you get on SSI, you lose a job) or you move, then notify your debt collector immediately. Make sure the proper paperwork is attached to your file and your address is correct. You'd be surprised at how much incorrect information can get attached to your account.

# CHAPTER 23

## HOW TO OVERCOME CREDIT CARD DEBT?

**N**ow, if you already have your credit cards and you have incurred expenses greater than your income, of course, the monthly payments will be difficult to cover without affecting the budget necessary for the maintenance of your basic expenses such as variable expenses which are vital to your livelihood. It is at this moment that you will require the design of a plan to get out of the debts that afflict you so that it does not affect your requirements and you can recover your credit history.

In that sense, you can consider the following suggestions if you want to get out of your credit card debt:

You should suspend the use of credit cards, especially those that demand higher interest payments. Do not hesitate to use scissors to cut them for safety and freedom is better not to have what will not be used.

Of course, you should not stop paying the monthly installment of your credit cards and if necessary, to achieve this end go to the financial and banking agencies to request the renegotiation of the debt being able to agree on monthly payments that can amortize the debt.

If you have extensions of your credit card you must eliminate the temporary or definitive use of those credit cards to your relatives or associates, all will benefit above all your credit history.

You must give priority to your expenses and if necessary, for your job only allows you to have the credit cards that yield greater benefits and you can get offers in cases of having to travel exclusively for work.

Since you cannot finance your card payments on time and your income does not allow it, opt for alternative jobs that allow you to earn new income. Don't make the mistake of incurring new debts to pay the one you already have.

The sumptuous and leisure or recreation expenses that you usually add to the credit on your cards should be suspended for the duration of the credit recovery or payment of delinquent debts.

At the moment of undertaking again the use of the credit cards investigate and inform yourself properly of the interest rate, the taxes that require and use those that are of your utility, at this point always less is more.

The commitment you make to your credit history is yours alone and your responsibility, so don't think that there will be magic solutions to get you out of the excesses committed.

Remember, the recovery of your credit history will depend on the degree of commitment you have, controlling your finances. You must program your expenses making a budget where you can, according to your income, distribute the payments of your expenses.

If you delegate this function you will not change your consumption habits and therefore you will continue with uncontrolled expenses that put you at risk and prevent you from recovering your credit history. Above all, don't pay a credit repair agency to do work that is solely your responsibility, and these agencies often use illegal or unreliable tactics. Maybe you could end up having more problems than benefits.

Limit the use and opening of accounts in stores as this negatively affects your credit rating in the short, medium and long term. Uses only credit cards obtained at financial and banking agencies of wide credibility. Also, consider not using more than one-third of your line of credit unless you're sure you can afford to pay it in full that same month. Do not leave debts for the next few months, thinking that you will be able to pay it with an income that is not fixed.

Many companies pretend to offer free credit reports but charge for their monitoring services. These companies encourage you to sign up for a free report, ask for your credit card and automatically switch you to a paid service after a trial period. Therefore, if you do not cancel your subscription within this period, you will be charged every month for their services.

If you need specific information about local credit reporting agencies or other aspects of credit ratings where you live, check with the relevant agencies in your country.

The financial reality is changing in each country and of course the economic conditions in some countries can sometimes be unfavorable especially for micro and small business entrepreneurs, as they cannot access bank loans, are forced to resort to informal lenders, weakening their financial and economic capacity, because the interest rates they charge tend to rise steadily, often exceeding the rates of return generated by their businesses, and instead of helping to grow, often ended up decapitalizing them. In the face of this, it is preferable to turn to trusted individuals or state entities for credit support or refinancing.

# CHAPTER 24

## WARNING SIGNS OF CREDIT CARD ADDICTION

Is there such a thing as credit card addiction? Can someone really be addicted to using these plastics that have exorbitant interest rates? The answer to both of these questions is "Yes". Credit card addiction and compulsive shopping are interrelated, because many compulsive shoppers use their credit cards to pay for their purchases. This is depicted in the movie Confessions of a Shopaholic, where the heroine is a compulsive buyer who ends up acquiring too much debt on her credit cards. The situation looks funny in the movie, but having a lot of debt that you have no way of paying can get you in a lot of trouble in real life.

Credit card addiction is the overwhelming desire to buy things that you may or may not need using your credit card. This can potentially ruin your finances in the end, because when your debt starts to build up, your income will no longer be enough

to pay for it and you will end up bankrupt. Compulsive shoppers use credit cards to feed their shopping obsession. This is because it is more difficult to spend hard-earned cash that you have in your wallet than to spend borrowed money contained in a plastic card.

To be able to treat your credit card addiction and eliminate debt, you first need to know if you really have the condition. You need to observe your credit card usage to identify potential red flags that could mean shopping addiction using your credit card. If you can observe any of these warning signs, you may be suffering from credit card addiction:

- Frequently buying things that you do not really need is one red flag that you need to look out for. Because of this, you end up with a lot of stuff at home that you do not really use and only end up collecting dust at the back of your closet or under your bed. You are also tempted to buy unnecessary items just because they are on sale.

- When you hide your purchases from your spouse, parents, or other close family members, it could also be a sign that you have credit card addiction because you know that what you are doing is not something to be proud of. You know that you are doing something wrong, which gives you that guilty feeling and is the reason why you hide your purchases.

- Another warning sign is when most or all of your credit cards are maxed out, which means that you have reached your credit cards' limit and you can no longer use them to make purchases unless you pay at least the minimum.

- You are also in trouble if you just keep on paying the minimum every month. Paying the minimum prevents you from getting a late fee, but what it actually does is it doubles the balance that you need to pay.

- You also need to watch out for other less acute warning signs that can ultimately lead you to a lot of debt. Check out the list below:

- Using your credit card to purchase everyday items, even those that only cost a few dollars, is also an indication of a possible credit card addiction. Paying for small groceries, gas, dollar meals, a pack of cigarettes, and other inexpensive items is not a good idea because once these items add up, you will realize that you have already acquired a lot of debt without buying anything major.

- Not paying your full balance every month can also lead to credit card addiction because it gives you the feeling that you can get away with not paying the full balance. Later on, you will only pay the minimum and before you know it, you have accumulated a large debt on your credit card.

- People who ignore their credit card statements because they are afraid to look at their bill also display signs of credit card addiction. This means that you have done something that has dire consequences, which is why you are afraid to view your credit card statement.

- When you are juggling several credit card bills, and you are skipping one bill to pay off another, or you are making cash advances from one credit card to pay

another, then it is possible that you have credit card addiction.

- Some people also rely heavily on their credit cards to pay for things that are not in their budget. This can also be a sign of credit card addiction. For example, if a designer bag is definitely not in your budget because you cannot afford it with your income, but you are still going to buy it because you have a credit card

- Another sign that indicates that you are heading towards credit card addiction is when you have several past due accounts. This means that you have been using your credit cards, but have not been able to pay even for the minimum fee.

- There are also those who are habitual buyers and returners. They buy things compulsively only to return the items the next day because once they arrived home, they realize that they do not really need or like the item. They just cannot control their urge to shop using their credit card.

- There is also a condition called "retail therapy" where people, go shopping to make themselves feel better when they are in a negative mood. If you are like this, then you should be wary of your behavior because this can be a sign of credit card addiction or compulsive shopping.

Once you have assessed your behavior involving your credit cards and realized that you actually have credit card addiction, the first thing that you need to do is to calm down and not

panic. You need to understand that this problem is common and you are not alone. There are also a different ways that you can stop your credit card addiction and eliminate your debt for good.

However, for now, you need to understand the negative effects of credit card addiction and compulsive shopping on your physical and mental health, emotions, relationships, career and life in general.

# CHAPTER 25

## HOW TO ELIMINATE UNNECESSARY EXPENSES?

Eliminating your unnecessary expenses can help a lot with your credit score. If you are not controlling your expenses, it will affect your payment history and that is about 35% of your credit score. This may lead to sometimes when you will have difficulty affording your minimum payments monthly and have missed or late payments. But if you will not control your expenses, and you have paid late, it will surely have a negative effect or impact on your credit. So you will have to consider things when using your credit card. So how will you eliminate unnecessary expenses? Here are some tips to keep in mind:

# Know Where Your Money Is Going

Always take note if that certain thing is worth your money. Just be certain that you prioritize your needs first. Lower the cost of your lifestyle. Everything counts, yes, every penny. If you are not aware of where your money is going, then that is the time that you will have to make yourself aware that you are now spending a lot. One tip is for you to jot down everything you buy up to the last of your money. Include your extra expenses, even the snacks you have bought. Keep track of what you spend every month; have a spreadsheet, ledger, or anything that may help you track everything every month.

# Remove Immediately Routine Purchases That Are Unnecessary

This one is easy and important. We will go straight to the point. Stop buying that coffee when you are on your way to work. You can make your own at home and it is much cheaper. Stop buying sodas one by one, you can buy it in a pack at a store and is much cheaper. Stop seeing movies at cinemas, you can watch them online. These are just some tips. It may hurt at first, but it will be a great help for you to save. You should consider having a grocery list instead, then go to the grocery. Only buy what is needed and listed.

# Have A Cut On Your Utility Expenses?

This one is very self-explanatory. When you are away from home, always remember to turn every appliance off, and when you leave a certain room, never forget to turn off the

light. Make use of bulbs that are energy efficient, it works. Turn off your laptop when not in use, no matter how it is uncomfortable to you. Save money, save water. Control the flow of the water you are using. Remember that every drop of it counts. Do your laundry as often as possible. Control your use of data on your mobile phone. Avoid engaging in having unlimited text if you are not really a person who needs it to text from time to time, or you may apply for cellphone plans.

## Control Your Fashion And Entertainment Costs

Ask yourself "do I really have to watch this new movie now?" or can you watch it after a few months for free on the Internet, or buy a DVD copy? Same as with your fashion. Do you really need to buy a bunch of clothes if you only have to make use of some?

You see it all comes down to a person's lifestyle. You should always consider the payments you will have to make after you have bought these things. Ask yourself at the end of the day, "Is that worth my money?" Have a self-evaluation and see for yourself.

## How To Leave Good Debt On Your Report?

Nothing feels better than earning your bank and credit card company's trust in you as a credit card holder when it comes to dealing with your debts and improving a good credit score. Leaving a good debt means that you have managed your account very well and paid the amount of debt you owe as

contracted, giving you a good reputation on your report. The longer the list of paid debts and credit history, the better the credit score. To pay your debts on time depends on how you weigh your budget versus your debts and accomplishing the payment agreement is an advantage.

## Steps On How To Achieve It

Want to achieve a good credit score and establish a creditworthy image? Why not power up an increasing boost on that three-digit number of yours? All it takes for you to improve your credit score is just simply being a disciplined individual who is able to use a credit card appropriately. Here are the contributing factors on how to have a good credit score:

- Do not overuse and misuse your credit card by splurging on a swiping spree. Remember, having a high credit score does not depend on how often you use your credit card, but how disciplined you are on paying your debts.

- Refrain from owning multiple credit cards. You may have small amounts remaining on each of the credit cards you own, but that does not add up to a small amount you are going to pay. Having for example, $70 on your card and $100 on another does not do your credit score any good.

- Always remind yourself to owe the least amount of debt as possible!

- Mark your calendars for the scheduled date of debt payments or set the important dates of payment on your mobile phone. To eliminate your debts on time is the greatest foundation to improve your credit score and

make a good report of your credit record, because not paying your debts on the scheduled date, even if you're late for only a day or two, leaves a negative record on your credit score.

- Manage your budget expenses by setting aside the allotted money to pay for your debts.

- Always pay your debt expenses right on time, and when you do, be sure to communicate well with the bank you have an account with, to let the company know that you are paying the credit, or for confirmation purposes that you've paid a certain amount of debt already.

- Keep the amount of the debt you owe low and pay your balances on time. Avoid stacking up debts which will give you a hard time paying as agreed.

- Do not get anywhere near the maxed-out limit! Make it a habit to maintain a low amount of credit card balances to avoid having the poorest credit score.

- Be consistent in handling your debit/credit card accounts properly when it comes to maintaining a good credit score, so as not to ruin your record.

## How To Not Hint At Risk?

Having a bad credit score record will cost you so much. It ruins your reputation as a money borrower, and because of that, moneylenders and creditors see you as a risky cardholder; you might not even be able to borrow money at all. A bad credit score affects so many bank benefits and loan approvals. The poorer your credit score, the higher the

interest rate you are going to pay.

But you can always get back on track. You can win back your good credit score, and here is what you need to do.

## Steps On How To Achieve It

### Manage your balances

Always maintain a low credit card balance and keep your remaining credit high. A high amount of debt affects your credit score. Using your credit card too much will not give you a good credit score. Lessen your credit card balances. Creditors may mistake you as a desperate cardholder.

### Pay your credits on time

Simple as that. Be a responsible credit cardholder. Pay your bills on the scheduled date. Late payments and unpaid credits strongly contribute to a bad score.

### Check your credit history report

You cannot start anew if you do not know how to boost your score. Request a copy of your credit score report. Find out the accounts that affect your credit score. Manage the accounts that pull your credit score down.

### Correct any report errors

Credit reports are not always accurate. If you find some errors on your report, it is your right to have the inaccuracies corrected. Notify the creditor who recorded said account on your report too so he/she can make the corrections. Write a request of removal to your credit bureau and have it fixed.

### Communicate with your credit card issuer

The more you get left behind on your payment dates, the more it lowers your credit score. 35% of what makes up a credit score amounts to your payment history. Before your payment is too late, talk to your credit card issuer. Before the company charges off your unpaid debts, ask the lender to re-age your debts.

Re-aging means restarting your time to pay for your debts before they are collected. Re-aging fixes a poor record because your account will appear as though you are paying debts on time. Eradicate a late payment from your report. This will save your credit score. It takes a great deal to re-age a debt so communicates well with the issuer.

**Do not open multiple accounts**

Do not make it a habit to own multiple credit cards. Credit card inquiries will not make you a responsible cardholder. 10% of your score amounts to credit card inquiry. The more you inquire about credit cards, the lower your score. Just apply for new accounts when necessary.

**Do not close unpaid accounts**

Too stressed on the amount of debt you owe. Closing your credit card account is not a solution to solve unpaid debts. Make sure to pay your credit balances before closing an account. If not, this will definitely ruin your credit score.

# CHAPTER 26

## BEST WAYS TO SAVE

## Build A Savings Account

The two most common types of checking accounts that most people have are checking and savings accounts. By keeping money in a checking account, you can gain easy access to that money for spending by writing out a check or swiping a debit card. A savings account is a little different. Many people put money into a savings account for the purposes of, obviously, saving. You might open a savings account to save money for emergencies, retirement, or a down payment for a large asset.

Money that you put into a savings account acquires interest over a period of time. Best of all, you don't need a large amount of money to start a savings account. Depending on your bank, you might only need as much as $25 to begin. Some banks charge a low monthly fee or offer them for free

to open a savings account and interest rates will vary by bank. Always shop around before deciding on a bank to open a savings account with. You should generally be able get one for free.

There are many benefits to opening a savings account. First and foremost, your chances of spending that money are much less than if your money was in a checking account. Secondly, your money is safe in a savings account. If your house were ever to get burglarized, or if a tornado ripped through your neighborhood and swept your house away, your money would still be safe and sound in the bank. Money in a savings account is also safe because it is insured by the FDIC if you live in the USA. So if your bank were to close, you wouldn't lose your money. Finally, many people open savings accounts to accrue interest. That is when your bank pays you money to lend your money. When that happens, your bank will usually pay you interest every month.

Basic savings accounts, which usually only re□uire small fees to get started, only earn a small amount of interest each month. A market money account gains a higher amount of interest but often has limitations. For example, you need a lot of money to put into it, and you can only make a small number of withdrawals.

Once you've opened your savings account, your bank will give you a log where you can track your money. You can also track your deposits, withdrawals, fees, and interest gains by reading your monthly statements.

# The Simplest Ways to Save Money

Now that you know what to do in order to get a handle on your finances, it is time to learn about little, easy things you can do to save money. Sometimes, saving money is as easy as making a simple switch or thinking about your alternative options.

Fold it, put it in your pocket, and keep it there

One of the best and most commonly Ⅾuoted advice about saving money is this: "The best way to double your money is by folding it in half and putting it in your pocket." In reality, literally folding your money bill in half won't double its amount. However, the total value of what you have can and will be doubled for each day you follow this habit successfully. If, for example, each day you set aside five dollars without touching or scheming to spend it on something, by the end of the week, you would have added 35 dollars to your savings.

How It Helps:

Folding your money over or simply keeping it in your pocket won't just save you some money, it will help control those shopping impulses. One of the most common mistakes people make when they get their money on payday is splurging. It's no surprise if you can relate to a scene like this: Payday arrives and you feel as rich as a king. It only takes a week, or less, of seemingly endless wealth until you're broke or nearly broke. By the end of the month, you're sulking, cutting down expenses and waiting at the edge of your seat for the next payday. The cycle happens, and it will continue to happen over and over again until you decide to act upon it.

## Saving Every Penny

Most people think of small bills as insignificant because, well, they are small or have less value and would not really be of any use in emergencies. The truth is, they are actually the most significant portion of the idea of "savings."

How It Helps:

Small amounts are what a person builds up and turns into millions. Mountains are not made of singular gigantic boulders. They are made of sand, stones, rocks, and some boulders. In the financial comparison of mountains to savings, it's the pennies that make up the base and not the hundreds. While saving pennies won't make you rich, it will change your relationship with money. If you practice putting your coins in a tin every day, you will condition yourself to save. This brings us to the next overlooked technique in saving money, for long- or short-term purposes.

## Starting Small and Starting Now

Starting small is the easiest way to save, but starting small is belittled by most because of the expected value it achieves. "Every little bit counts," that's one saying that applies to a lot of things, including saving money. Since the idea of saving up is a continuous and consistent habit, even the small contributions add up to the pile. It's also easy to save by starting small because it gives people enough freedom to buy the things they need or want. It won't feel like such a responsibility, which will lengthen its chances of actually growing to be a successful habit.

## Investing Your Money

Besides opening a savings account and letting the bank lend out your money, there are many other smart ways to invest your money. This will give an overview of the different types of investing. Many people are turned away from the idea of investment because it can often be a risky venture. However, as long as you go into it with knowledge and goals, your chances of being successful can be higher.

1. Invest in Property
2. Invest in Other Businesses
3. Capital Gain Incomes
4. Invest in Stocks
5. Invest in Bonds
6. Real Estate
7. Assets

# CHAPTER 27

# FEATURES OF A GOOD CREDIT REPAIR COMPANY

Enlisting the help of a Quality credit repair company may end up being one of the best things you have ever done for your financial future. A good credit score can improve so many aspects of your life from the home you live in to the car you drive to the job you work. But choosing a bad company not only won't get you any closer to achieving your credit goals, but it could lighten your pocketbook or worsen your credit situation.

Below is a checklist of things to look for when shopping for a credit repair company you can reference to help you separate the trustworthy companies from those that are better left alone.

## Length of Time In Business

Starting a credit repair business is easy. There are several software programs you can purchase that will essentially allow you to create a new company overnight. What these programs don't provide, however, is expertise.

Your credit score is too important to trust to someone who isn't an expert at credit repair. As a general rule, you will be better off selecting a company that has been in business for a few years. Not only will they have more experience, but there is a better chance that they will remain in business for years to come.

A company's BBB profile is a good resource for seeing how long a company has been in business. If a company does not have a BBB profile, they may be too new or unknown

## Upfront Fees

The Federal Credit Repair Organizations Act states "no credit repair organization may charge or receive any money or other valuable consideration for the performance of any service which the credit repair organization has agreed to perform for any consumer before such service is fully performed." This provision was put in place to protect consumers from companies that would charge hundreds or even thousands of dollars for services and then either not providing the agreed-upon services or not be able to positively affect the customer's credit report, something that is a possibility no matter how good a company is — be leery of a company that reⓊuires a payment before providing services.

## Physical Location

Having a physical location speaks to the company's stability and intention to provide services on a long-term basis. A company that does not provide a physical address or only has a PO Box is more likely to disappear once they have your money. Also, make sure to plug-in the company's address in a service such as Google Maps so you can see the actual building. It is not uncommon to find that the address is a personal residence which

## Payment Options

At a minimum, a credit repair company should accept credit cards, preferably by processing them themselves instead of using a third-party service such as PayPal. This allows you to take advantage of your credit card company's fraud protection services if necessary. A company that only accepts cash, checks, or money orders is probably one that you want to avoid.

## Breadth Of Services

When credit repair companies first started, their services consisted solely of generating credit bureau disputes. This method can be useful in cleaning up a credit report, but it tends to be slower does not work in all cases, and only addresses the 35% of a person's credit score that has to do with derogatory listings.

Today, the most successful companies provide additional services such as goodwill letters, direct creditor disputes, debt validation, and credit score coaching. Make sure you find a

company that offers the services necessary to help you achieve your credit goals.

## Option To Choose Which Items To Dispute

There are two reasons why this is important. First, the Credit Repair Organizations Act forbids companies from making claims that are untrue or misleading which "upon the exercise of reasonable care, should be known by the credit repair organization" such as disputing a negative item you know is accurate. Second, there are times when disputing a negative item is a bad idea such as when it is an older item or represents a legitimate debt that has not been paid. Disputing these items can actually result in a lower credit score.

## Too Good To Be True Promises

Legally create a new credit report, guaranteed 700 credit score, permanently remove all negative information form a credit report; these are all promises that are too good to be true for a reason. Not only is it impossible for a company to guarantee that they will be able to positively affect your credit score, it is illegal. The same is true of creating and trying to get approved for credit using a new credit report.

# CHAPTER 28

## HOW LONG IT TAKES TO OVERHAUL YOUR CREDIT SCORE

**W**ith the right strategies and an aggressive, determined mindset, you could go a long way toward improving your score in 30 days. You could even be able to improve your score by 100+ points, which is quite phenomenal.

It is true that you can make significant headway in a month. However, how long will it take to really turn your credit around and have it in an excellent state? How long will it take you to fix your credit completely so that the unpleasant items disappear completely? From a realistic standpoint, how long will a complete overhaul take?

The answer to the questions is certainly not 30 days. Even a couple of years would be ambitious unless you either had

very few negative items in place or somehow successfully applied to have every negative item on your credit report removed.

Credit revisions usually take time. Some people think that if you dispute everything on your credit report, you will somehow compel the bureaus to revise your credit. However, it is pointless to dispute accurate information on your report. If you indeed made 3 late payments in the last financial year and your creditor reported this, all a dispute will do is waste your time, the bureau's time, and that of the creditor—and the negative item will still reappear next time.

## The 7 Year Limit

Typically, most negative items take 7 years to age off and fall off your report with the exceptions being bankruptcies and unpaid tax liens that often hang around for at least a decade.

With this said, you do not have to sit passively and wait for the negative items to fall off. One great strategy to have the negative items removed, especially if you have since paid off the outstanding amounts, is to write to your creditor and request to have the item removed. It is true that a mere request may get you your desired revision (they call it goodwill), but it is likelier that you will have to settle for some financial settlement or other, in order for them to remove the negative item. Nevertheless, expect the process to take some time, since your creditor may insist on checking your recent financial record to determine if you deserve having the item taken off your report.

## Steady Improvements Should Contribute To The Bigger Picture

With all of this said, while you may have to wait several years to see a total overhaul of your credit situation, you could see significant, marked improvements every few weeks, especially if you combine the credit repair strategies with responsible credit handling.

Here is a strategy that will help keep your credit score improvement consistent. Since the typical American is obsessed with his or her credit card, ensure you keep your credit utilization at 30% or below. Let us now look at how to ensure that your credit health remains great.

# CHAPTER 29

# How to Protect Your Credit Card From Identity Theft

dentity theft is an existing crisis in the US that's continuing to grow every year. An Identity Theft Resource Center (ITRC) report is quite disturbing. It shows that 1,579 data breaches exposed about 179 million identity records in 2017.

How identity theft can ruin your credit score

The most common type of identity theft crime is credit card fraud. Fraudsters would steal your personal information and your credit card details. They would then use the stolen information for unauthorized transactions.

The fraudsters can either steal your credit card or perform a card-not-present fraud. But, they'd also need information such as your birthday and Social Security number.

You may end up with a credit card bill that you might not be able to pay or handle if you become a victim. This may affect your credit score if you don't act on it fast.

# Ways To Avoid Becoming An Identity Theft Victim

Proving that you're a victim of identity theft can be inconvenient. There's a long process to go through which involves a lot of documentation before you can prove your innocence.

It would still be best to avoid these kinds of troubles and there are several ways you can do it.

1.  Watch out for Phishing Scams

A phishing scam is a criminal's method to get personal information such as passwords. The most common way of phishing is sent via e-mail.

These e-mails would look like official e-mails from a bank or other companies. The contents would often inform you about system changes or promotional offers. It would ask you to enter personal information because of these reasons. In some cases, these e-mails scare you into providing info by saying that that access to your account will be restricted if you don't "update" your account.

The e-mail would also contain an external link to a fraud web page that would look like the bank's legit website. Entering your personal details on this page will result in big problems for you. The criminals will use your details to perform transactions under your name.

You can avoid being a victim by remembering one important rule: Banks generally will never ask for your information. If you absolutely have to make sure you need to update your account, contact your bank first.

To avoid these scams, stay updated with the latest phishing scam techniques. An updated browser and firewalls also help to prevent phishing scams.

There are also anti-phishing toolbars available online. These will alert you if you visit a suspicious website.

2.  Protect your computer data

Defrauders can also get vital information about you by hacking your personal computer.

They can use a keylogger that records everything you type on your computer. They may also intercept your Internet traffic and record information you send online.

People who transact online are the most vulnerable to these kinds of attacks. But, there are various ways to safeguard your computer data from hackers.

You must use a firewall and set a password for your WiFi. You should also install reliable anti-malware software. Many hackers use malware and other viruses to get information from computers.

Also, make sure that you're using secured connections. Public WiFi connections aren't secured, so it's best to avoid using them as much as possible.

3.  Protect your passwords

Using passwords is one of the ways that keep accounts safe. But, not using them properly would still make you vulnerable to identity theft.

Your password must be strong and not guessable. Shocking as it may seem, many people use "password" and "123456" as

their passwords. These are actually the weakest passwords anybody could use.

Avoid using birthdays, phone numbers, or other personal information as your password. It's best to use a combination of numbers, letters, and symbols. In this way, your password will be difficult to crack.

However, highly-skilled hackers may still be able to get your password. Using multifactor authentication especially for online banking might add security to your accounts. Some banks, for example, require that you confirm a transaction by using a temporary pin sent to your registered phone number.

You must also have different passwords for your accounts. If one of your accounts gets hacked, all your other accounts would likely be vulnerable as well.

The most important thing to remember is never to share your passwords with anybody.

4.   Protect your mail

Imagine all the information an identity thief could get from your mailbox.

Criminals do not only steal information online. They can also get your personal information from the mail you receive if they find a chance.

To avoid mail identity theft, start by cutting down the amount of junk mail you receive. This includes insurance and credit offers.

You should also keep mail with important information in a locked container. If your mail is piling up, you can shred them

instead.

For incoming mail, you can either get a locking mailbox or a P.O. Box. The locking mailbox looks like a normal mailbox, but it can only be opened with a key A. P.O. Box may be safer than a locking mailbox, but you'll need to pay for it monthly.

For outgoing mail, you must avoid putting it in a mailbox especially if it contains checks or cash. As an alternative, drop it off at the post office or in a collection box. You may also hand it directly to a mail carrier.

But with today's technology, companies now offer paperless bills. This will not only prevent mail fraud, but you may also get some small bill discounts.

5.  Protect your credit card number

As mentioned above, fraudsters can use your credit card to perform unauthorized purchases. All they want is the credit card number and your personal information.

The basics of securing your credit card start with your signature. Sign the back of your credit card as soon as you get it. Also, don't write and keep your pin in the same place where your card is.

Keep your credit card safe by not letting anyone in public see it. Sometimes, you may receive calls from your "bank". Unless you made the call, never give your card information.

You must also watch out for phishing scam e-mails from your bank. Even if it looks legit, don't give your personal details or credit card number.

It's also a good thing to update your bank information

regularly. Update your phone numbers and e-mail address as soon as changes occur. Also, be up-to-date with fraud alert systems and respond immediately to notifications.

Lastly, report lost credit cards or any fraud activity suspicions right away. Your bank can block your account and credit card to avoid others using it.

6. Spot unauthorized credit card charges quickly

It's essential to check your credit card statements on a regular basis. Many unauthorized charges can go unnoticed for months if you don't do this.

Review your statements early and check for any purchases that you didn't make. If you don't report it ASAP, your credit card issuer will not give you much time to dispute. Also, you might end up being liable for the charges.

Call your issuer immediately once you spot an unauthorized charge on your account.

Once your credit score is tainted with a bad record, it's difficult to fix it. You may need to endure a negative credit score for some time before you can recover from it. Protect your personal information and educate yourself about the new scams criminals develop. Always remember that these criminals will never stop finding ways to get what they want.

We don't live in a perfect, crime-free world. You must be vigilant at all times to protect your interests. You don't have to fall victim to identity theft.

# CHAPTER 30

## ERRORS TO AVOID WHEN STARTING A BUSINESS

**M**aking marketing work for your organization you have to understanding when to hire new workers and when to let nonperformers go. Taking benefit of offered resources and staying organized, you can discover the lessons related to starting and growing your organization in 2 methods. The very first is by making the mistake and after that tidying up the mess afterward. The second is by observing others' errors, gaining from them, and then not making them yourself. For you, we've made and observed numerous of the mistakes we're about to talk about. After all, why go through the pains of experimentation when you can get what you require from the experiences of others like us?

1. Failing to Use Financial Statements to Manage Your Business

A sensible old sage as soon as said that if you can't measure it, you can't handle it. That declaration is definitely real in-service. Your organization's financial declarations (the supreme in measurement) can supply all the info you require to make the finest decisions, when managing your organization. Too many small business owners think that, since they can take a look at the bottom line of the profit and loss statement (P&L) and locate the net earnings figure, they know whatever they need to understand about their financial declarations. They neglect such tools as the balance sheet, cash flow declarations, cash flow projections, and spending plans, together with myriad valuable percentages and ratios that progress from all those monetary declarations . Every business transaction creates a number, and every number adds to a story that gets informed within the pages of your financial declarations.

Therefore, a secondary function of generating financial declarations is to utilize them to assist inform your employees on how the business works, with the underlying purpose of motivating them to do what they can to enhance success. In the event that you need to choose to offer your service, no sophisticated buyer will think about purchasing a company that doesn't produce precise and professional monetary statements.

2. Failing to Prepare an Annual Budget.

Budgeting is among the most underrated, underutilized, and yet potentially valuable tools offered to the small-business

owner. The budgeting process is a detail-oriented, tiresome discipline, and yes, it's stuffed with assumptions, however the advantages. You enjoy establishing an annual budget make the process eminently worthwhile. The 2 main advantages you receive from developing a budget are.

Precise preparation: A yearly budget is truly nothing more than a forecasted earnings and loss statement for the upcoming year. Making the necessary assumptions is always the most difficult part of preparing a budget plan. Some of the presumptions are simple to make (believe rent, office materials, and telephone services), while others are more tough (believe overall profits, gross margins, or profitability). The only way to create the best assumptions is to prepare for them, hence precise preparation is a requirement for accurate budgeting.

## Expenditure control

Expenditure control is a cultural concern, and a company's culture is identified by the leader, which implies that the small-business owner is ultimately the one who determines whether or not the organization will bear in mind its costs. The very best way to start establishing an expense control culture is by adopting a zero-based budgeting system as you develop your yearly spending plan. (Zero-based budgeting methods that at the start of every year you start with zero and justify every dollar of every expenditure rather of simply including a fixed percentage.

Planning and managing expenses through budgeting not just impact success; however also play an important function in

managing capital. Every dollar you save by planning to lower your phone bill collects in your examining account. You will not discover a better, or much easier, way to begin building a healthy, cash-positive service than by managing costs as long as those costs do not negatively affect your services or product, obviously.

3.    Failing to Utilize Your Certified Public Accountant.

Make no error about it: Among the disadvantages of a small-business profession is that it can be among the loneliest careers. That isolation usually leads small-business owners to guide their businesses alone, as opposed to their Fortune 500 equivalents, who have their boards of directors and layers of management staffers to assist them make.

Decisions. A minimum of one individual in your working environment has the background and knowledge to assist you in directing your business; that individual is your Certified Public Accountant, or whoever prepares your organization's tax returns. What makes your Certified Public Accountant so important?

Nobody can provide conclusive recommendations on how to run a service without first understanding and applying the info created by monetary declarations. Most Certified public accountants have experience dealing with other small business owners and their financial statements, most CPAs who prepare monetary declarations for small business owners are small-business owners themselves. Certified public accountants know how to prepare taxes correctly, which makes both you and the Internal Revenue Service delighted. While Certified public accountants don't precisely

offer away their time, you don't have to give a leg and an arm to get a little consulting advice. Ask your Certified Public Accountant to tack on an hour to the end of your yearly, year-end tax evaluation.

4.  Stopping working to Understand How.

Marketing Applies to Your Company, every small-business owner confronts a variety of marketing misconceptions over the course of her profession. These misconceptions tend to puzzle and misinform small-business owners, not only in the pre-start-up phase as they set out to develop their marketing plan but also as they graduate into handling the sales and marketing function of their continuous business. The following are primary among these marketing misconceptions: Marketing is everything about business and promotion.

Sales is a stand-alone function, separate from marketing from the list in the preceding bullet, you can see that the " sales" activity is however one of the 9 functions of marketing.

Granted, it may be the most observable of those functions it's no more essential than any of the others, especially customer support.

5.  Hiring Too Quickly.

Why are most small-business owners so fast to employ? What makes this task so difficult? The main reason is that employing brand-new staff members falls under the classification referred to as human resources, a category that consists of tasks associated with the management of people in a company. Although you 'd much rather develop a brand-new

product or contact a consumer or (we hope) evaluate your financial statements, handling individuals is one of the needed evils of developing and constructing a company, and hiring is a crucial element at the same time. To comprehend just how essential hiring is, attempt attaching an expense to its failure. If you work with a nonperforming staff member, the expense will equal the expense of the errors that make sure to follow, plus the expense of the left employee's lost training time, plus the time and energy needed to start the employing process all over again.

To improve your hiring skills, follow these two basic guidelines:.

- Always location employing at the top of your to-do list, and leave it there until you have actually effectively accomplished it.

- Employ gradually. Take your time. After you make the hire, undoing it is expensive.

6. Taking Too Long to Terminate.

Nonperforming Employees, if we had a nickel for every time we've heard a small-business owner state something like the following, we 'd be rich! " Sure, I know it is a headache, but I can't fire the man. He's been around too long." And then, 2 weeks later he was lastly fired and the organization is running so much more efficiently now, he would've fired him five years back." Within 30 days after working with an employee, the majority of small-business. Owners can identify whether or not they've made an error. Yet, they wait another six months, or perhaps five years, to do something about it. The

underlying reason for this far-too-frequent mistake is that small-business owners prefer to invest their time doing the things that they enjoy and are skilled at doing, so they procrastinate doing unpleasant tasks. Not surprisingly, firing isn't an satisfying activity for most service owners and the majority of individuals aren't competent at it, but it's as essential to the success of an organization as any of the other three team-building functions hiring, training, and motivating.

Businesses that do not eliminate the bad workers are at greater risk for losing their high-performing staff members to services that much better recognize and reward the best and dismiss the worst. The nonperforming employee who remains on a company's payroll not only takes excessive of management's time however likewise drags down the remainder of the group. Those workers who are performing start to feel bitter the worker who isn't performing; right after that, the group's performers likewise start to feel bitter the company owner for permitting the slacker to continue his employment.

7. Presuming Your Workers Are Inspired by the Exact Same Things You Are

Why do not my staff members do things the way I would do them?" is the normal small-business owner's lament after another employee has actually failed to solve a client's issue, neglected to act on a designated task, or eliminated of the parking lot exactly at five

o'clock, leaving behind a desk stacked with incomplete work. Ask any veteran small-business owner and she'll quickly tell you that a vast majority of her work environment

aggravations evolve from an inability to comprehend why her workers do what they act the method and do they act. In other words, staff members drive small-business owners nuts.

The primary factor for this owner/employee detach is easy: Workers aren't motivated by the exact same things that small-business owners are. (This distinction is typically for the very best. After all, can you envision what your company culture would be like if all your employees were like you?) While the typical business owner is motivated by such things as growth, creativity, and independence, the typical worker is encouraged by such things as being part of a group, having issues solved, and sensation protected. The 2 lists are entirely different. Provided the severe difference in inspiration in between the owners of organizations and their employees, is it any surprise that workers respond to situations in a different way than their owners would choose them to respond?

8.   Thinking about Training Cost and Not an Investment.

Envision that you own a small organization and your incomes are growing at a rate of 25 percent a year. For a lot of individuals, that sort of development would be an exciting and positive pattern, yet it can mask a variety of risks (such as costs that grow too quickly or too many slow-paying customers) to the unwary small-business owner. To avoid those risks, you and your essential workers need to be growing at a similar, or much faster, rate as your organization.

# CHAPTER 31

## SETTING YOUR EXPECTATIONS: LIFE AFTER BANKRUPTCY

Undergoing confusion and frustration accompanied by filing for bankruptcy, you may feel as if your life is never the same. Of course, financial challenges will change most of your viewpoints and perspectives in life.

A change in lifestyle sums up the aftermath of bankruptcy. First of all this is the best solution that you should pursue towards recovery. Fortunately, there are many proactive ways of dealing with this drastic change.

Make sure that you are willing to change your perspectives and tone down your expectations. So what happens then after bankruptcy? What kind of expectations should you set in order to recover eventually?

Let's start with legal matters. First, if you filed a Chapter 13 bankruptcy, you'll undergo a process called "reorganization".

This is a result of your discussion with the court about how much you need in order to live, and working with a trustee to distribute your money among your creditors.

This process, though stressful, is still for your benefit. Yes, you'll still be paying some of your debts after the proceeding but under manageable terms now. This process takes at least three to five years to be completed.

Second, if you filed a Chapter 7 bankruptcy, you are essentially debt-free save for some exemptions like child support.

Keep in mind that bankruptcy would not save you from obligatory expenses or financial responsibilities. While your debts may be forgiven, the bankruptcy you filed stays in your credit report for 10 years.

For each of the bankruptcy types, there are specific ways for you to adjust in order to rebuild your life. For Chapter 7 more especially, you will have to rely on cash instead of credit.

If this is the circumstance, you should focus your expectations and inclinations towards earning hard cash and managing it properly.

For both types of bankruptcies, you will be rendered a risk among lenders.

If you're viewed as a risk, you will generally have difficulty securing credit (this is why it is not advisable to get credit cards too soon or incur credit post-bankruptcy).

And when you do get credit, it might come with higher-than-the-average fees and rates. Why?

Post-bankruptcy, your debt-to-income ratio income increases. This ratio measures the amount of debt that you have against the amount of money you make. In effect, since filing for bankruptcy puts all of your debts upfront, the total amount may exceed your income.

Credit companies will look into this and in order to make sure that they can make profit off you, they will charge higher fees and rates which may even put you deeper into debt and financial struggle.

Generally, lenders consider 36 as an acceptable ratio. The lower it is, the better chances of you getting credit.

Consider your credit ratio first before thinking about loans or credit. Apart from working to improve your credit score, you can also start monitoring your progress by looking at how your debt-to-income ratio increases over time.

Do not be hasty about accepting credit offers or loans. It may be tempting with respect to your situation, but it is very important to consider the right timing before you make any financial decision. At the moment, delayed gratification is a better choice for you.

Some key points for you to remember:

1. **Acknowledge that there are no rules of thumb in credit re-building**

There are several ways to regain a good credit score, but there are no exact rules that you need to follow in order to achieve this.

The best way to rebuild your credit depends on your specific situation and what you can accomplish given your resources.

You probably have come across other books or articles online that tell you exactly how you should approach the post-bankruptcy lifestyle.

The truth is that there's not a perfect strategy to get past the challenges in life after bankruptcy.

At some point, you would have to undergo trial and error while keeping on remembering what your financial obligations are post-bankruptcy.

What exists though is your commitment to rebuild not only your credit score but your life as well.

### 2.   Positive attitude matters

Above everything else, a positive attitude will give you the initiative and the motivation to fulfill the tasks that you need to regain your positive credit score.

A good attitude will increase the chances of you recovering during post-bankruptcy.

You might still have a considerable amount of money, or you might belong to the high-income bracket of society, but if you settle with destructive behaviors, things may become more challenging for you.

### 3.   Live a changed life

You probably have learned a lot following the bankruptcy proceedings so now is the time to put those insights into practice.

There is no other way to recover during post-bankruptcy other than thinking of action steps and putting them to practice.

The best way to do this is to incorporate it into your lifestyle. If you still have a credit card, you know that you should use it wisely.

If you have bills to pay, you know that you should pay those on time. What's important is getting accustomed to this new life. You'll end up getting better at money if you do.

Finally, the key towards surviving following discharge from bankruptcy is living simply. Know what it means to have a lifestyle that is considerably minimalist and not gregarious. Know what important expenditures are versus non-important ones.

That means sticking to the basics in spending and not spending more than you can pay. Keep in mind what your true buying power is, considering your debts and all of your financial obligations.

To live simple means to know what your priority is when it comes to spending. You may still spend money on your wants and luxuries, but know the proper limit with respect to your financial priorities.

So what you're thinking applies here: it's a life with a no-frills policy but offers a rewarding sacrifice in the end. What steps can you take to restore your life once again?

# CHAPTER 32

## HOW TO FIND A REPUTABLE CREDIT COUNSELOR

C redit counselors can be an enormous help if you're in the unfortunate situation of having no way to make all of the payments that you owe on time. If your only other alternative is bankruptcy, they can help you avoid that by helping you to come up with a plan to manage and pay down your debts responsibly. They can also help you with contacting creditors to figure out a mutually agreeable solution, among other things. Basically, they're there to help you dig yourself out of this hole, to help you weather this storm.

The mere act of getting credit counseling will not hurt your FICO score. It's what you do as a result of that counseling that can hurt it. So choose your credit counselor wisely, and avoid damaging your credit by implementing wrong-headed advice.

The trouble is, there are too many greedy scammers out there who make a living by preying on desperate people. I don't want you to end up as one of their victims, so here is how you sidestep them and find a credit counselor that you can trust.

One more thing. Although the use of a credit counselor will not hurt your FICO score, if the use of a credit counselor shows up on your credit report, future lenders may frown upon it, worrying that if you needed to resort to using a credit counselor, you aren't able to manage your debts as agreed upon.

So only pursue this route if it's the lesser evil — for example, if your alternative is bankruptcy, and credit counseling can help you avoid that, credit counseling would likely be the lesser evil.

## Government Recommended Or Sanctioned Credit Counseling Agencies

Anyone can make a slick website that looks professional to trick you into thinking you can trust in their expertise. The good news is, you can easily weed out the scammers by only considering those agencies that are recommended in some way by the government. Here are a few that you should take a look at.

1.  Hope Now

Hope Now is an organization that was formed via an alliance between credit counselors, mortgage companies, and other participants in the mortgage market. This alliance was encouraged by the US government to help create solutions

that would solve mortgage problems. They help troubled homeowners find solutions that will allow them to stay in their homes. If you've made some late payments on your mortgage, or are at risk of missing any, take a look at what Hope Now can offer you. Here is their website: www.hopenow dotcom.

2.  The National Council of State Housing Agencies

These guys can be a great help in providing you with support for any housing finance questions or concerns. You can search by state to find the agency nearest you. Check out what they can offer here: www.ncsha.org/housing-help.

3. HUD-approved Counseling Services

HUD-approved counseling services can provide you with advice on defaults, foreclosures, and general credit issues, among other things: https://apps.hud.gov/offices/hsg/sfh/hcc/hcs.cfm

4.  The Department of Justice

The Department of Justice also has some great tips for finding reputable sources of credit counseling: https://www.justice.gov/ust/credit-counseling-debtor-education-information

## Credit Counselors Vetted By Professional Or Consumer Organizations

Next, take a look at credit counselors that have been vetted by professional or consumer organizations.

1.  The National Foundation for Credit Counseling

The National Foundation for Credit Counseling is the oldest non-profit financial counseling organization in the United States, with a focus on providing free or affordably priced services. They can be of help with a diverse range of credit problems, including:

- Credit/debt counseling
- Bankruptcy counseling
- Housing counseling
- Reverse mortgage counseling
- Student loan debt counseling
- Debt management plans
- Credit report reviews
- Financial education

2. The Financial Counseling Association of America

It represents non-profit credit counseling companies. They can be of help with the following:

- Bankruptcy counseling
- Credit counseling
- Credit report reviews
- Debt management plans
- Financial education
- Housing counseling
- Reverse mortgage counseling
- Student loans counseling

The National Foundation for Credit Counseling is the oldest non-profit financial counseling organization in the United States, with a focus on providing free or affordably priced services. They can be of help with a diverse range of credit problems, including:

- Credit/debt counseling
- Bankruptcy counseling
- Housing counseling
- Reverse mortgage counseling
- Student loan debt counseling
- Debt management plans
- Credit report reviews
- Financial education

2. The Financial Counseling Association of America

It represents non-profit credit counseling companies. They can be of help with the following:

- Bankruptcy counseling
- Credit counseling
- Credit report reviews
- Debt management plans
- Financial education
- Housing counseling
- Reverse mortgage counseling
- Student loans counseling

that would solve mortgage problems. They help troubled homeowners find solutions that will allow them to stay in their homes. If you've made some late payments on your mortgage, or are at risk of missing any, take a look at what Hope Now can offer you. Here is their website: www.hopenow dotcom.

2. The National Council of State Housing Agencies

These guys can be a great help in providing you with support for any housing finance questions or concerns. You can search by state to find the agency nearest you. Check out what they can offer here: www.ncsha.org/housing-help.

3. HUD-approved Counseling Services

HUD-approved counseling services can provide you with advice on defaults, foreclosures, and general credit issues, among other things: https://apps.hud.gov/offices/hsg/sfh/hcc/hcs.cfm

4. The Department of Justice

The Department of Justice also has some great tips for finding reputable sources of credit counseling: https://www.justice.gov/ust/credit-counseling-debtor-education-information

## Credit Counselors Vetted By Professional Or Consumer Organizations

Next, take a look at credit counselors that have been vetted by professional or consumer organizations.

1. The National Foundation for Credit Counseling

## Beware of Debt Settlement Plans

Beware of debt settlement plans where you pay a lump sum to a company that purports to "help" you by holding onto your money, without making any payments to your creditors, until they agree out of desperation to stop hounding you. The companies that offer this service may say you'll get off easier with a smaller payment and save money in the long run, but even if they pull this off, essentially holding your money hostage instead of making payments can trash your credit score.

You're better off trying to work with your creditors to come up with a payment plan that you can maintain, and that results in them getting the money they are owed. Everyone is happy that way, and you'll minimize or prevent any damage to your credit score.

## Beware of Unscrupulous Credit Repair Companies

These guys sound great — who wouldn't want someone to "repair" their damaged credit, right? The problem with many of these companies is that they try to fix your credit by challenging all of the negative things on it — anything that is not verifiable in the legal timeframe will be removed in as little as 30 days. Perfect, right?

Not really.

Because what happens is that the credit bureaus will continue to try and verify the challenged information — and if it turns out that the info they removed was, in fact, accurate, it'll be put right back on your credit report just like before.

And worse, if you successfully applied for credit based on a credit report with missing information (due to those challenges filed on your behalf by the Credit Repair Company), you could be charged with fraud. Because you can be held legally responsible for any action you take, even if it's on the advice of a credit repair company.

Additionally, credit repair companies can be expensive. And finally, you're risking identity theft by sharing your credit history with a stranger. The credit repair industry is not well regulated, so the credentials of whoever you end up dealing with may not be reputable.

As you can see, dealing with a credit repair company is a potential disaster in the making, and best avoided! The thing these guys don't want you to know is that the best way to repair your credit permanently is to do it yourself or with the help of a reputable credit counselor from a source.

## The Pitfalls of Starting Over With a Brand New EIN Number

Another illegal ploy sometimes suggested by disreputable credit counseling and repair companies without a conscience is that you start over with a brand new EIN number for all credit applications going forward. The idea is, you stop using your old social security number, and use a brand spanking new EIN number instead, which won't have all of your previous bad credit history on it. But this could take you into hot water with the law, so aside from being dishonest, it isn't worth the potential legal hassles that will likely ensue from it.

Remember, there are far better, legal ways to improve your credit score, even if your life has fallen apart and you're starting out with a disastrously low credit score.

## Do These Things First Before You Hire a Credit Counselor

There are a few things you should always do before hiring a credit counselor.

First, contact your state Attorney General's Office and local Better Business Bureau to find out more about this particular credit counselor's reputation. Also, ask if there are any complaints against them, and whether or not they were resolved.

Secondly, find out what kind of fees you'll be expected to pay for their services.

Thirdly, find out how and when your creditors will be paid — get this information in writing. You need to know this information so that you can follow up and ensure that they do what they say they will do.

Lastly, if credit counseling is a last-ditch effort to avoid bankruptcy, it might also be worthwhile to consult with a lawyer who specializes in bankruptcy proceedings, to discuss other legal options. They can also be a great sounding board for any suggestions that the credit counseling agency has made to you.

# CHAPTER 33

## CHARGEBACKS

So now you're looking at your credit card statements and watching over everything when you suddenly don't recognize a charge. After investigating for a bit to make sure it's not something you just forgot about, you realize that it's a charge that you want to dispute.

If there's a product that you bought online and you never received it, you can dispute the charge. Obviously, you also are never on the hook for charges made fraudulently on your card. If you are within a merchant's refund timeframe, you can often win the dispute automatically once you provide proof you never received the goods that you purchased. This is yet another reason why it pays to stay vigilant. Don't wait until it's past the merchant's refund time.

But, if your request for a refund is met with crickets or you are dead certain that this is not a charge you made, now it's time to get the credit card company involved. You're going to request what's called a chargeback. You must act fast because, according to the Fair Credit Billing Act, you only have 60 days from the day the disputed charge appears on your statement. Your credit card company has 30 days for you to respond, and they are obligated to resolve it within two billing cycles that take no more than 90 days.

 You may also want to take the extra step, which practically guarantees you'll win the dispute, by providing a letter to your credit card company's dispute department address. Include all paperwork, including copies of your statements, any emails, phone records, or confirmation letters provided to you. List out clearly and concisely, typed up neatly, exactly what happened. You're stating your case, that you deserve to have your money back and to win the dispute. As with other letters, make a copy and send it certified return receipt with a greencard through the mail. After the credit card company decides you're the winner and the merchant is the loser, then the merchant loses their charge amount and they have to pay fees. Merchants don't want to do this because it affects their credit history with the bank. The shoe is on the other foot now, isn't it?

The vast majority of customers win credit card disputes. The odds are stacked in your favor, especially with purchases that are backed by refund policies and guarantees. Credit card companies are certainly on the ball when it comes to fraud, so they might even notify you before you find that suspicious

charge.

Another way to win credit card disputes? This is one of those could-work-but-you-don't-want-to-test-it-too-many-times sneaky rules. If your credit card isn't physically present with you when it's being used, thus leaving a swiped-and-signed paper trail, then you win the dispute automatically. Serial chargeback artists abuse this loophole. Their trick goes like this:

Say someone used your card to book something online, and you two were in completely different locations. You decide to dispute the charges within a short timeframe, perhaps because of buyers' remorse or some other personal reason. You do have a legitimate claim to win your dispute because you weren't there when the card was swiped. This happens more often than you would ever guess in bars, casinos, strip clubs, and all the other All-American shady businesses.

This doesn't mean you should go around disputing every purchase on your credit card that was made by your buddy living two houses down, just because you weren't there to sign off on it. Credit card companies and merchants are getting savvier. However, it does go to show that the chargeback process is designed to protect innocent consumers even if a few scammers get free stuff, rather than the other way around. Don't feel bad about initiating a chargeback if you have been ripped off, double billed, or have charges you didn't authorize. However, you typically won't be able to do business again with any company you charge back with, provided they know who you are.

You're just one customer amongst the millions that your credit card company deals with each and every day. Act fast to stick within their time limits, provide all the paperwork if requested, and work with them. They'll wipe that amount off your credit card and keep your credit score from sinking as fast as your trust in that scamming merchant.

## The FDCPA Borrower Bodyguard

Debt collecting is a multi-billion-dollar business, and there's so much misinformation out there. Creditors and borrowers are locked in a nasty struggle over paying back loans, credit cards, and credit lines. You might feel as if you're penalized no matter what you do, that companies will hike up your interest rates, reduce your credit limits, randomly change the amount of your minimum payments, or harass you with ugly phone calls at any time day or night.

 But the laws around debt collecting have changed drastically in the last twenty years, due to not only the 2008 financial crisis but the collective mounting debt that Americans owe. As the borrower, you have more protection than you might think. You are not only protected by the FCRA (Fair Credit Reporting Act), but also the Truth in Lending Act and the FDCPA (Fair Debt Collection Practices Act).

The FDCPA is kind of like a borrower's bodyguard. It's a federal law that places strict limits on debt collectors who are attempting to collect your debt. Every time you're on the phone with creditors or collectors, and every time you receive a piece of mail from them, the FDCPA is working in your favor and protecting you. It seeks to find and eliminate abusive,

deceptive, and unfair debt collection practices. If a debt collector harassing you is found to be in violation of the FDCPA, then you can bring a lawsuit against them and make big money. How can you use this to your advantage? By knowing what they can't do.

Debt collectors can't mislead you, trick you, compel you, or otherwise coerce you into paying more than you owe. If you know for sure that you owe $8,000 and they're claiming $10,000, then ask to see their paperwork. Go over it carefully, preferably with an attorney. If the collector asks you to pay more interest, fees, or other miscellaneous costs that aren't allowed by law, they're also violating the FDCPA.

Probably the biggest advantage you have as the borrower is taking debt collectors to task on how often they call you. It's considered harassment. There are specific and strict phone regulations within the FDCPA as well, that have to do with autodialers and appropriate times to call. They can't call before 8:00 am or after 9:00 pm in your time zone. Also, if you've specifically stated that there are certain times during the day you can't be called and they do, then that is also considered harassment. Collectors cannot call your workplace unless you specifically request them to. Debt collectors cannot discuss your debt with anyone else who's not authorized unless you have specifically named them as the person to speak to. The only person they can talk to is your spouse. If you have an attorney and it's on your file with them, then they can't discuss the account with you. They have to speak to your attorney.

Threats are fairly common in the debt collecting industry. Collectors will tell you that you'll get sued, you'll get arrested, your wages will be garnished, your taxes will be taken from you, you'll lose your job or your vehicle or your house, or your credit will be permanently ruined. If debt collectors use obscene, profane, or abusive language, make these threats, or in any way deal with your account in an unprofessional way, they've violated the FDCPA.

Within five days of the first communication, the collector is required by law to send you a debt validation notice, which includes the amount of the debt, the name of the creditor, and letting you know you have 30 days to dispute. No letter, and they're in violation of the FDCPA. If they ignore your written request to verify the debt within 30 days of that notice and continue to collect on it, they have violated the FDCPA.

If any of this happens, take action immediately. All phone calls at the debt collections center are recorded. Let the collector know they are in violation of the FDCPA, you will be reporting it to an attorney, and you want a supervisor to listen to the call. If you're trying to settle the debt within a particular payment schedule or plan, you can use this as leverage. Please keep all records and paperwork to provide a nice strong case against the collector. You might be able to settle a large debt for 50% of the balance or even less, but make sure it says "paid in full" on your credit report. The language they use matters on the credit report!

You can also take it further. You can file a complaint with the FTC at their website: www.ftccomplaintassistant.gov. The FTC oversees debt collector actions. You can also file a complaint

with the Consumer Financial Protection Bureau (CFPB), which passes your complaint to the creditor and works between the two of you to find a solution. To submit your complaint: www.consumerfinance.gov/complaint.

Hiring an attorney to help you fight debt collectors either in state courts or small claims courts is a great option. You still might have to pay a large amount to settle the debt, but at least you won't be continuously harassed and threatened.

# CHAPTER 34

# THE SECRETS TO SUCCESSFULLY GET RID OF DEBT

*"Attitude is a little thing that makes a big difference."*
Winston Churchill

The small details that most people overlook are often the deciding factor in whether or not you'll be successful with your goals to get rid of unwanted debts.

So what's the big secret to success? You've got to lay out your goals in a very specific way and have the right mindset. I know that sounds overly simplistic at first glance, but stick with me.

### Cultivating the right mindset is crucial

None of this will work if you don't have the right mindset.

First, don't fall for the whole "money is the root of all evil" thing.

Some people feel guilty at the thought of having lots of money. They've been taught that only selfish, greedy people are well-off — and since they don't want to be that kind of

person, they self-sabotage by making bad decisions about managing their finances.

But having money isn't necessarily bad or good — it's how we use it that makes it one or the other. For example, if right now you're deep in debt, you probably can't afford to donate to charities that are important to you. But imagine how different it would be if you were firmly on the road to financial freedom, out of debt, and had money to spare — you could do so much good with that money now that you finally have enough of it. You could donate to causes that you believe in, help deserving family and friends, and so much more.

Additionally, if you take care of yourself financially, your loved ones won't have to stress out worrying about how you'll afford to take care of yourself. And you won't have to worry about it either.

The key takeaway is that having money is good if you put it to good use.

Second, understand that even if you stink at managing your debts right now, you can change.

Research proves that we are capable of changing ourselves. So even if you've always thought of yourself as being prone to getting into too much debt, this doesn't mean you're destined always to be that way.

### Third, go into this for the long haul.

It's very important that you go into this with the expectation that it'll take time to get rid of your debts. The last thing you want to do is feel down because "it's taking too long". It's normal for it to take significant time to get rid of debts, so

don't beat yourself up over this reality, okay?  Also, if bad spending habits are what got you into debt, remember that it's normal for it to take time to change them. According to a 2009 study published the European Journal of Social Psychology2, it can take anywhere from 18 to 254 days for a new behavior to become a habit.  Don't let the "up to 254 days" depress you though.  I know that's a long time to wait for new attitudes and behaviors surrounding money to become habit, but, as the saying goes, "better late than never".  And remember that some people were able to change their habits in as little as 18 days — maybe you'll be one of them!

In any case, a key takeaway is that you can create new and better habits as long as you persist and give it enough time to become automatic.

So whatever you do, don't quit too soon.  And no matter how many days it takes your new ways of handling money to become natural, it's not as though it'll be all bad in the meantime — you'll still be making a lot of good decisions on your way there.  And if you mess up, just dust yourself off and assess the damage, then come up with a plan to keep going in the right direction.  Don't quit.

### Now it's goal time

Once you know about the eye-opening research that's been done on goal setting, you'll be able to use this knowledge to dramatically improve your success rate with reaching your objectives for debt reduction and ALL other areas of your life.

Here are the small but powerful changes you need to make to maximize your odds of success.

## S.M.A.R.T. Goals

If you want to set goals that you're actually going to accomplish, they need to be SMART, and have the following five characteristics.

1. Specific

Your goal should be easily understandable, not too broad, and have enough detail to make clear exactly what you mean.

Bad: Pay off debts.

Good: Pay off the $3642 owing on my Sears credit card within the next 2 months.

2. Measurable

Your goal needs to be measurable, so it's completely obvious whether or not you've reached it.

Bad: Save money.

Good: Put aside $500 in my savings account in the next 3 months.

3. Actionable

Ensure that your goal includes an action that you can take to attain it.

Bad: Save money on groceries.

Good: Cook rice as a side dish three times a week instead of using potatoes (which cost more per serving).

4. Realistic

Your goal needs to be something you have the skills, knowledge, and ability actually to do.

Bad: Win the lottery.

Good: Increase income by applying for two part-time job openings every day until I land one of them.

5. Time-bound

Whenever possible, include a deadline in your goals. This helps to prevent your goal from slipping away into the indefinite future.

Bad: Pay off my mortgage.

Good: Pay off my mortgage within 5 years.

But while ensuring your goals meet as many of the above criteria as possible is an excellent start, it still isn't enough if you want to maximize the odds of success completely. To find out how to do that, keep reading.

## The 3-Step Secret Recipe For Success With S.M.A.R.T. Goals

Okay, so this may not be a secret by the strictest of definitions, but since most people don't use this recipe for success, it might as well be a secret. According to research, people who follow the recipe I'm about to share with you have a much higher chance of attaining their goals compared to people who don't. And there are three major components of this recipe which we haven't covered in our previous discussion of SMART goals.

First, after you've written down your goals, jot down an "action commitment" for each one. For example, if your SMART goal is to "Increase income by applying for two part-time job openings every day until I land one of them," your action

commitment could be "Spend 1 hour per day finding job openings in my local newspaper and Craigslist that I can apply for."

Here's another example. If your goal is, "Pay off the $3642 owing on my Sears credit card within the next 2 months," your action commitment might be,"Sell my car to get the money required to pay off Sears credit card (and use public transportation instead of driving my own vehicle)."

And here's one more example for you. If your goal is "Put aside $500 in my savings account in the next 3 months," your action commitment could be "Stop spending $6 per day on a large Frappuccino at Starbucks for 84 days, and put that money into my savings account instead." (84 days x $6 per day saved = $504 cash saved up)

The second thing you need to do is share this goal and commitment with a friend.

And the last thing you need to do for this "secret" recipe for goal success is send a weekly progress report to your friend. This will hold you accountable.

The study compared goal setters who used some, or none of the above three techniques — the most successful were those who used all of them.

## A Big Caution

Don't skip a single part of the above recipe for success. Because if you do, it'll probably make you less likely to achieve your goal. Here's why: in an interesting study, researchers asked law students about their desire to make use of educational opportunities. Those who expressed a goal to

make the best use of such opportunities were divided into two groups. One group had their desire to reach the goal of making best use of educational opportunities noticed by an observer, and the other group was able to keep their goal to themselves.

It turns out that the group who shared their goal spent less time, on average, making use of educational opportunities that were subsequently presented to them. Researchers theorized that this may have been because sharing their intentions to make the most of these opportunities created a "social reality" of sorts. That is, sharing the goal made it seem a bit like it had already been reached, so they didn't try as hard to make the most of it.

## The solution

So how do you get around this? You create goals that are SMART (specific, measurable, actionable, realistic, and time-bound), you share them with someone, and you build in accountability by sharing progress reports.

You'll notice that in that study, the "goal" wasn't very specific, it wasn't measurable, nor was it time-bound. The lack of those three important parts of a SMART goal could be why sharing the goal wasn't enough to help them increase the odds of success. Additionally, there was no accountability process baked into that study.

I suspect that those law students would have done better if they'd created a SMART goal along with an action commitment such as, "I will study law for four hours a day, six days a week for 12 consecutive weeks, in addition to going to

all required law school classes during that time period", plus shared the goal with the experimenter, and submitted weekly progress reports.

So when you're creating SMART goals for paying off your debts, ensure that all of your goals are specific, measurable, actionable, realistic, and time-bound. Don't forget your action commitment. Plus, when you share them with a friend, be sure to commit to regular progress reports that will put pressure on you to actually do what you set out to do in the first place.

## One goal you must include on your list

One of the most important goals to include on your list is to stop borrowing more money. Because if you fail to stop, you're merely digging yourself into a deeper hole that'll be harder to climb out of. Formulate a SMART goal in regards to stopping the borrowing cycle, and ensure that you use the above recipe for success to make it happen.

## A note about credit cards

Here is an important point that you need to be aware of if you use credit cards. If you have any credit card debt that you don't pay off in full each month, you should stop using your credit cards until you 100% pay them off, and come up with a plan to ensure that you'll never, ever, rack up credit card debt again.

# CHAPTER 35

# CREDIT REPAIR POSITIVE AFFIRMATIONS

1. I am debt free.

2. Wealth and abundance pour into my life on a regular basis.

3. Money is flowing to me right now.

4. I have a large bank balance at all times.

5. My life is filled with one success story after another.

6. I am successful at everything I do.

7. Everything I touch turns to gold.

8. I am wealthy, I am wealthy, I am wealthy.

9. Every day is a wealthy day.

10. Being financially secure brings me joy and happiness.

11. I am receiving all that is good.

12. I celebrate being wealthy.

13. I am able to treat myself every day with the things I love.

14. I can walk into a shop and buy whatever I want.

15. I can afford to shop in the most expensive places.

16. I have great success and wealth.

17. I believe I have the right to be rich.

18. I manifest wealth, success and abundance.

19. Being rich is easy.

20. Everything I need comes to me easily and effortlessly.

21. I love and appreciate money.

22. I am financially rewarded for the work that I do.

23. I am an open channel of creative money making ideas.

24. I am open to receiving all the financial blessings the universe has to offer.

25. Every day I am growing more financially prosperous.

26. It is ok for me to have everything my heart desires.

27. I am always in the right place at the right time.

28. I give thanks for my wealth, success and abundance.

29. I create money miracles.

30. I love giving and I love receiving.

31. I feel inspired to make money every day.

32. I am able to express my money making ideas freely.

33. I am rich and powerful.

34. I am able to train my thoughts on abundance easily.

35. My wallet is overflowing with money.

36. I am an abundant person.

37. Financial abundance is mine for the taking.

38. Financial abundance is mine and I accept it now.

39. I always have more than enough money.

40. I always find ways to make large sums of money.

41. I am focused on achieving wealth and success.

42. I let go of all resistance and allow money to flow into my life easily.

43. I release my fears and worries about money.

44. I find it easy to attract money into my life.

45. I naturally attract great wealth into my life.

46. I am highly focused on achieving financial success.

47. My mind is in harmony with the energies that create wealth and abundance.

48. I am getting more and more used to the idea of being wealthy.

49. My financial situation improves on a daily basis.

50. Money appears in my life through many channels, and in harmonious ways.

51. I attract many lucrative circumstances into my life.

52. All the money I spend brings me joy and happiness.

53. Financial freedom makes me feel content and secure.

54. I live in an abundant universe that constantly supplies me with everything I need.

55. I am the creator of my own success.

56. I am living an abundant, rich life.

57. Having money makes me feel great.

58. I release all resistance to money.

59. I enjoy being wealthy.

60. I am getting more and more prosperous as each day passes.

61. There is a wealth of abundance available to me and I accept it now.

62. An abundance of money is always circulating in my life.

63. I always have more money coming into my bank account than going out

64. I accept money from all positive sources.

65. I naturally attract money to me in many different ways

66. My money consciousness is always increasing.

67. I am surrounded by money.

68. I allow money to flow into my life consistently and easily.

69. I am grateful for all the money I have.

70. I put 100% of my energy into my financial goals.

71. I find it easy to set financial goals and achieve them.

72. I am gracious for the wealth and success I have in my life.

73. People love to give me money.

74. I am earning a fantastic income doing what makes me very happy.

75. All of my bills are fully paid each month with more than enough left over.

76. A lot of money is coming to me today, and I deserve it.

77. I spend money wisely and happily, blessing myself and others.

78. I am richly paid for the work that I do.

79. I always make smart financial decisions.

80. I give generously to myself and others.

81. I run a very successful business.

82. My business grows stronger every day

83. I attract dozens of paying customers through my door every day.

84. I have several successful businesses.

85. I have a great business mind.

86. My business grows from strength to strength.

87. My business is very profitable and lucrative.

88. My business makes me a lot of money.

89. I love the financial freedom my successful business provides.

90. Running my successful business fills me with excitement each day.

91. I attract successful businesses into my life.

92. I always win major business contracts.

93. I have excellent business contacts

94. I run my business easily and effortlessly.

95. My business always makes a profit.

96. My successful businesses always take me to beautiful countries around the world.

97. I run a successful company from the comfort of my own home.

98. My company is profitable and successful.

99. I am a successful businessman/woman.

100. My employees help to make my business the success that it is.

# CONCLUSION

C redit is significant for anybody's accounts. It gives an individual a history and reputation of their budgetary history. With credit, individuals can fund things, for example, a house or a vehicle. At whatever point an individual has credit, it is significant that they use it shrewdly. A decent record as a consumer will empower them to get low financing costs on credits just as can get more cash. There are various things that individuals should remember when utilizing credit. They should do things, for example, take care of tabs on schedule, check their announcements, check their credit reports and furthermore maintain a strategic distance from the base installment propensity.

Dealing with your record is significant on the off chance that you need to ensure that you can acquire enough cash to purchase a house or a vehicle. It will likewise enable you to get the most minimal loan costs and set aside you cash thus. At whatever point you are hoping to deal with your credit, it will be imperative to ensure that you charge a sum that you can

stand to pay back and take care of your tabs on schedule. This will enable you to build up and keep up a decent record of loan repayment and deal with

As you have read, after taking a fall, there are so many ways for you to rebuild and jump back into credit arena. The problem people tend to face after recovering is that there is always that latent desire to return to old habits. The idea that can go through your head when you're debating making a purchase may be, "Just one time I'll just use my credit card." Don't do it! This is the only time the old self will be allowed to start charging again.

You've worked hard with resettling and restoring your reputation to this level. It wasn't done overnight but now you're in a position where you should be worry-free.

Holding the accounts and finances in order is a cycle that continues for life. Regarding dieting, they say it's a change in lifestyle and the same goes for our finances. Not only will you feel good about your condition by changing your lifestyle and living within your means, but you can also serve as an example to your family and friends. Children learn how to handle their parents finances well. Chances are, if you're a good money planner, your kids will be when they're adults. Even if you've fallen on hard times, the kids will see how you've picked yourself.

The main thing to take away from this book is to make sure you've got a workable budget. This cannot be put enough emphasis on. It's getting out of your reach and not keeping track on what's going in and out that's going to set you off. It is a new practice worth learning about.

There are ever-changing new laws and regulations. Staying on top of any new changes is part of your new financial life. Please read the documents the bank and credit card firms are issuing. Even the small fine print you can barely read contains details that can change your credit terms and save you more money.

You can't be overly careful with your personal identification in today's society. It's too sad that we need to watch for unscrupulous people who want to exploit our identities and use them in all the wrong ways. At all times be on the lookout to defend yourself and the identity of your kin.

Go ahead, and give yourself a pat on your back. You deserve this. You're back on your feet now and you've learned from your mistakes. It's time to start working towards your milestones.

www.ingramcontent.com/pod-product-compliance
Lightning Source LLC
LaVergne TN
LVHW051224050326
832903LV00028B/2243